Praise for
DON'T GIVE IN!
(YOU'RE NOT JUST GETTING OLD)

"*Don't Give In!* is a heartfelt, humorous, and relatable journey through decades of evolving health trends, told with refreshing honesty and wit. For anyone who grew up in the '70s and '80s, it's a nostalgic walk down memory lane—and a powerful reminder that it's never too late to take control of your health.
"This book doesn't just inspire—it motivates. Halfway through, I was so moved, I put the book down and went for a walk.
"*Don't Give In!* is the encouragement we all need to stop settling for what no longer serves us and start showing up for our healthiest selves. You'll laugh, reflect, and walk away with renewed energy to keep going."

—Janice Litza, MD, FAAFP, ABOIM, program director, family medicine residency, All Saints Family Health Center

"I needed this book. I helped me highlight a few places where I need to do better and set me on a path of enlightenment. It helped to know that I wasn't the only one going through 'old age,' and I felt the author spoke as a friend."

—Tracey S., reviewer

"An easy read with a casual flow that felt like I was talking to an old friend. *Don't Give In! (You're Not Just Getting Old)* is an inspiring tale of how Kathy has turned her life around, starting with a history of her past difficulties and finishing with what she has done to take back her health."

—Danielle M., reviewer

"*Don't Give In! (You're Not Just Getting Old)* is a compelling blend of memoir, self-help, and health manifesto that challenges the pervasive narrative of inevitable midlife decline. . . . Combining personal anecdotes with practical advice, the book serves as both inspiration and a roadmap for women navigating the physical and emotional challenges of aging. . . .

"*Don't Give In!* addresses the interconnectedness of physical, mental, and emotional well-being. Bauernfeind emphasizes the importance of sleep, stress management, mindset shifts, and incremental habit changes—making her advice accessible and sustainable. . . .

"*Don't Give In!* contributes to the growing body of literature pushing back against ageist stereotypes, particularly for women. Bauernfeind's work aligns with the ethos of books like *Younger Next Year* but distinguishes itself through its memoir-like intimacy and rejection of perfectionism. It's a rallying cry for midlife women to reclaim agency over their health without succumbing to shame or unrealistic standards. . . .

"*Don't Give In!* is a heartfelt, pragmatic guide for women tired of being told their best years are behind them. Its strength lies in its authenticity and refusal to oversimplify the complexities of midlife health. While not a substitute for medical advice, it's a powerful tool for mindset shifts and sustainable change."

—Sarah J., reviewer

"What an interesting and honest woman Kathy is! I whizzed through this book, finding it a really easy read. I enjoyed the tales of her food, pot, and, poor thing, the shoulder surgeries when younger. And then reading about how she found the resolution to sort herself out physically. It's not a how-to book, more the tale of one woman who decided a plan of how she was going to sort her physical self out and went for it. As a woman of a similar age, I found it inspiring!"

—NetGalley reviewer

Don't Give In!
(You're Not Just Getting Old)
How an Average Middle-Aged Woman
Took Back Her Health

by Kathy Bauernfeind

© Copyright 2025 Kathy Bauernfeind

ISBN 979-8-88824-753-2

All rights reserved. No part of this publication may be reproduced, stored in a retrieval system, or transmitted in any form or by any means—electronic, mechanical, photocopy, recording, or any other—except for brief quotations in printed reviews, without the prior written permission of the author.

Published by

3705 Shore Drive
Virginia Beach, VA 23455
800-435-4811
www.koehlerbooks.com

DON'T GIVE IN!
(YOU'RE NOT JUST GETTING OLD)

How an Average Middle-Aged Woman Took Back Her Health

KATHY BAUERNFEIND

VIRGINIA BEACH
CAPE CHARLES

To my brother, Jim, whose charming story "Take My Trash, Please!" gave me the idea to share mine.
To those dealing with Meige, you are strong.

TABLE OF CONTENTS

INTRODUCTION 1

PART I: THE DAMAGE 3
Chapter 1: Food 5
Chapter 2: Cigarettes 13
Chapter 3: Alcohol 15
Chapter 4: Pot 18
Chapter 5: Shoulders 22
Chapter 6: Jaw 31

PART II: EARLY FITNESS ATTEMPTS 33
Chapter 7: Exercise Tools 35
Chapter 8: Health Clubs 37
Chapter 9: Tennis 39
Chapter 10: Swimming 41
Chapter 11: Skating 43
Chapter 12: Belly Dancing 45
Chapter 13: Fred Astaire 46

PART III: PREPARING FOR RECOVERY 47
Chapter 14: Reasons to Fight Back 48
Chapter 15: Weight 57
Chapter 16: Mind Work 61
Chapter 17: Tactics 67

PART IV: RECOVERY 77

Chapter 18: Physical Work 78

Chapter 19: Trainers 87

Chapter 20: Training Places 91

Chapter 21: Breaking Barriers 103

Chapter 22: Food Work 113

PART V: NEVER GOING BACK 133

Chapter 23: The Tipping Point 134

Chapter 24: A Note on Choices 137

Chapter 25: A Note on Reverence 138

Chapter 26: Patient, Slow, Steady: Forever 140

APPENDIX A: Shoulder Surgery Survival Tips for the Single Person 141

INTRODUCTION

I almost ruined my life with excess. What I put into my body, how I used my body, and how I thought about my body. I ate too much of everything, and what I did eat was junk. I smoked a ton of cigarettes, drank a ton of alcohol, and smoked a ton (a *ton*) of pot. I spent most of my adult life overweight, with a bloated stomach that made me so uncomfortable and unhappy that sometimes all I did was lie on my bed feeling miserable. I also overworked my body and, between 1997 and 2011, had five shoulder surgeries and developed a slightly misaligned right jaw.

I was fifty-five, overweight, and tired. My body *hurt*. I thought I was just getting old. But a quiet voice wondered if feeling this way was inevitable, and I found my way back into the sunlight of feeling healthy and happy and alive again. Now, at sixty-six, I'm sharing my journey. It took me ten years to save myself. If others feel miserable and hopeless and want to make a change, maybe I can save them some time.

PART I

THE DAMAGE

Yet another evening found me sitting on the couch in front of the TV, exhausted, bloated, and miserable. Each day was the same, and they were all passing me by. How did I get here?

Of Benjamin Franklin's thirteen guidelines for living a good life, the first is temperance: "Eat not to dullness; drink not to elevation." If he'd been around 200 years later, he might have added "Smoke cigarettes not to hacking" and "Toke not to stonage." Unlike Benjamin, I lived my life trapped in a prison of excess.

CHAPTER 1

Food

It all started with food. I grew up in the sixties and seventies amid all the wonderful new "food": Twinkies, Oscar Mayer bologna and hotdogs, Wonder Bread, Tang, Hostess Cupcakes (*ah*, that wonderful white filling and squiggly topping), SpaghettiOs, Swanson's TV dinners (the cherry cobbler *always* boiled over into the peas), Chef Boyardee pizza in a box, Lay's potato chips with Henri's French Onion dip, Hamburger Helper, Pop-Tarts, Kraft Mac and Cheese, and the new phenomenon: McDonald's.

I'd get home from school, grab two Twinkies, and breathlessly wait for the next episode of *Lost in Space* to see if Don would finally notice Judy—even though they'd been living on top of each other in the spaceship for how long? No one knew.

I'd crush potato chips in a small plastic baggie into granular gold (a.k.a. fat) and, oh joy, eat it with a spoon. I'd eat a whole box of Kraft Macaroni and Cheese meant for a family. And three scoops of rainbow sherbert were never enough. (My mom asked me once what I was "trying to do to myself." Support the rainbow sherbert industry, I guess.) Every Wednesday I used the chocolate chip recipe in my 1968 *Betty Crocker's Cookbook for Boys and Girls* while waiting impatiently for *Medical Center*, starring dreamboat Chad Everett.

Classic chocolate chip cookies aside, I look back and wonder why my mom bought all that stuff because neither she nor my dad ate it. I guess it was for us kids, which would have been my brother and me, the last two of five. The only thing my mom and dad indulged in were Reese's while they watched TV nature shows in the evening. Smooth and creamy and individually wrapped in gold, packaged in two layers. As soon as they shooed me off to bed, I heard the faint crinkling of the wrappers and (of course) *always* found an excuse to go back down. I will forever associate Reese's with PBS and cozy evenings. Sixty years later, I still have a positive visceral reaction when I see Reese's in a store.

I've searched earnestly and exhaustively for evidence of some kind of childhood deprivation and find none, but I've always seemed to want (need) more of everything.

My aunt used to decorate her Christmas trees with homemade sugar cookies: Santas with red and white icing, green Christmas trees with yellow candles, and white angels. It's embarrassing and painful to admit how many of those cookies I snagged from the tree and devoured. I was a sneaky kid, pulling from different places, but anyone with observational skills could tell the tree was barer after I'd left (cringe). One evening, everyone was enjoying a bowl of ice cream, and, of course, I asked for more. Something inside me must have recognized the pathology, given I recall these incidents half a lifetime later.

I worked at Gimbels my last year of high school, in a mall with a new McDonald's. An immediate ritual was born: Filet-O-Fish before every shift. Four or five times a week. (I'm thinking of the *Simpsons* episode when Homer observes that, instead of eating his Filet-O-Fish, he should just slap it onto his thighs.) Even though the cheese was *never* centered on the sandwich, I ate a lot of those things (mmm . . . that tartar sauce). Sometimes two at a time.

I always felt like I needed to have a big meal. I came to realize when I began changing my health habits that I ate large meals for comfort, to remind me of the family meals we'd had when I was young: gathered around the faded green oil tablecloth in the warmly lit kitchen. The best meal was spaghetti.[1] Meals were followed by the new phenomenon sweeping family dinners: flaky cherry crescent popovers, hot from the oven, with the plastic tube of white frosting. (Lips were often singed because I couldn't wait one extra minute to bite in.) Full meals were connected to happy memories.

I temped at a large corporation in northern Wisconsin. It was a cutting-edge organization, one of the first to have employee wellness programs and a large full-service cafeteria with choice of entrées. I'd eat with some of the staff, and one remarked on the large amount of food I'd taken (what I thought of as a normal meal: meat, potato, vegetable, dessert, drink). She was a nice person and didn't say it in a mean way—more as an observation. I just smiled but did notice her lunch bag with one sandwich and an apple—and a slim body to match. A tiny seed was planted. Thank you, nice lady, wherever you are, for caring enough to say something. During that assignment, I'd go in on the weekends. "Word processing" had just become a thing, and I offered to work on a large mail merge project—an unfathomably marvelous technological convenience. I'm pretty sure I was the only temp who went in on weekends, but I was far from home, and it was part of my lifelong workhorse ethic. It's impossible to imagine days when a temp would get a pass for free access to a facility! Point is, even though it was only ten minutes from home, the first thing I had to do on arrival was stop at the vending machine for a 1,000-calorie artificial chemical ham and cheese sandwich. God forbid I should go an hour or two without sustenance. Sometimes I had two.

---

[1] The worst: chipped beef on toast.

I worked the evening shift in a law firm where I shared a desk with a mom whose sons were always selling something for school. The best (or worst, I guess) was the Reese's three-pack. Reese's, my emotional weak spot. My coworker (wisely) kept a supply in her drawer, and I'd drop in a dollar and grab a three-pack—on some nights, two or three times. In the space of a couple hours, I'd pounded 800 calories into my body. And that didn't include anything I might have for dinner. She also sold bags of an almond, coconut, dried banana, and carob mix. They were pretty big bags, and sometimes I ate two in an evening. Don't even want to guess how many calories were in those things.

Deep down, I must have known I was on a bad road because sometime in the mid-eighties, I signed up for a one-hour community class on stress relief where eating came up. I shared that I often ate large amounts of food even between meals. The instructor's suggestion that a couple of crackers and peanut butter would be a better choice struck me as absurd and showed how far into food I'd fallen. No concept of moderation.

Away at graduate school, I put on ten pounds in the first semester. I wasn't exercising, and my shoulder had dislocated (more on that later), so I really, really wasn't moving. Instead, I studied or smoked with my roommate and stress-ate Swanson chicken pot pies, Haagen Dazs butter pecan ice cream, and cheddar cheese. One morning I realized my jeans were so tight, my legs were literally throbbing. The school also had a full cafeteria, and I always felt the need to load up my plate: meat, potatoes, vegetable, roll, dessert, soda. And for the forty years or so between 1980 and 2020, despite whatever I'd had during the day, I always had a full meal for dinner. (One of my bosses casually mentioned one day that she was eating light because she was going out to dinner. I thought *that* was obsessive!)

When I temped at a visiting nurses agency in Dedham, MA, I stopped each morning at the Burger King drive-through for some kind of egg sandwich (and orange juice "to be healthy") and ended each day at the same place for a Whopper and onion rings. And when I temped at an engineering firm in Newton, I just *had* to start each day with a stop at the vending machine for string cheese, peanuts, and Fritos. Pure habit.

Between 2012 and 2016, I had a high-paced job as the grant manager at a large federal health center. Lunch was a greasy (albeit sensational) piece of pizza with garlic rolls or maybe something "healthy" from a local deli: a large turkey sandwich with chips, sometimes soup, and a cookie. In-between snacking consisted of Goldfish crackers and jars of dry roasted peanuts. And when I submitted large grants, as a treat, I walked to a nearby ice-cream shop for a scoop of pistachio and chocolate. And to top it all off, it was almost impossible to pass up stopping at Culver's for the fifty-minute drive home: cheeseburger, onion rings, strawberry shake: 460, 400, and 730 calories, 1,590 in one meal—two times a week (if not more). One pound of body fat contains anywhere from 3,436 to 3,752 calories.

I was pouring calories and chemicals into my body.

CHAPTER 2

Cigarettes

I started smoking around sixteen. I hadn't talked about it with my parents, but I wasn't hiding it and smoked at home. I only smoked in my room, but oh, how I cringe to think of smelling up their house. Two of my older brothers had too, so maybe they were resigned.

A quick cig between classes

In eleventh grade, I got suspended for smoking in school. The vice principal was surprisingly understanding, admitting that he smoked too and didn't know what he'd do without the teacher's lounge. My dad didn't get mad or punish me. His reaction was gentle (like he was), but I knew he was disappointed. I feel grateful that I didn't have harsh or abusive parents, but it does make me wonder if a harder approach would have veered me off the nicotine path. Being a typical teen, it likely would have only made me want to smoke more. As I write this forty-five years later, I realize they'd indeed figured out the wise way to deal with it. Makes me recall the admonition (that for years I thought was from Eleanor Roosevelt but is actually from Al Capone) to never mistake gentleness for weakness.

With my usual excess, I smoked addictively: at least a pack a day, reaching for one immediately upon waking. The first one of the day tasted great—the rest were never as good.

Smoking was exciting and felt so grown up. Going to the Folk Fair downtown with friends and lighting up while sitting high in the stands, we might as well have been in Europe! Heading out to a lake "with boys" with a whole new pack of Marlboro Greens (crystallizing your lungs with menthol made you especially cool). Feeling like I was an international traveler on the Orient Express taking the train to my brother's in Illinois and going into the four-by-four bathroom to finish one of my halves with "Got To Be There" playing overhead. Chain-smoking in a car with my aunt, uncle, and cousin to Florida and back—it must have driven them crazy.

It's amazing to consider how people used to smoke indoors. My first job out of high school was at a place where a man chain-smoked while editing appraisal reports. By the end of each day, his large ashtray was spilling over. He hated his job and must have felt forced to stay—so maybe he was trying to smoke himself to death. During breaks, we all sat around our supervisor's desk and smoked. One of the other editors was a frail, quiet woman who sat in between the man and us as we puffed and talked. I don't know how she endured all that smoke (and likely obnoxious chatter) eight hours a day. When temping in northern WI, my desk was at the end of a narrow hallway. I smoked all day but used to push my ashtray behind my typing stand. I must have started becoming self-conscious of the habit.

I'd tried quitting several times, sometimes more seriously than others, but never successfully. Going out with friends, I took sunflower seeds to eat instead of smoking cigarettes (I didn't make it through the first hour). I substituted pot for cigarettes (that didn't even work). I finally managed to quit for good in 1983 when I saw a man holding a voice box in front of the hole in his throat. Scared the *fuck* out of me. The bottom line about quitting smoking (and as I'd learn later about deciding to take back my health) was that the whole thing came down to a decision—no more, no less. (When President Eisenhower decided to quit, he "gave himself an order.") *Am I or am I not going to do this? I want to do this, I should, but am I going to?* Good health is not about some huge grand plan. It's about making one large decision and a steady accumulation of small ones. I decided to quit.

Like everything I do, I planned my quitting like a military operation: stocking up on sugarless Diet Root Beer and sugarless hard candy. (I have *no* idea how I decided on those two things. I'd never even had them. Maybe a subconscious desire to select something symbolically new and unfamiliar for such a monumental task.) It was Michael Jackson's "Human Nature" summer, and when I hear that song, I'm right back there on those hot summer evenings, pounding Diet Root Beer. I knew I was going to gain weight—nineteen pounds. But I also knew I had to tackle one thing at a time. I could always lose the weight. Only in the throes of withdrawal did I understand how insidious the smoking habit is: finding myself connecting cigarettes with happy childhood memories when I most certainly wasn't smoking. But the horror of seeing that voice box kept me going.

It took about three months for cravings to subside. It was like Dorothy stepping out of her house into Munchkin Land, like walking through a door into a brand-new life, like being somewhere I'd never been before. Some people describe quitting smoking as losing a friend. But it's more like meeting a brand-new person: yourself. A self you didn't know was there. It made me feel powerful and strong. It made me feel joyous.

Alas, twelve years later, in 1994, I started again in graduate school while sharing a dorm with my German roommate. Like any respectable European, she rolled her own, and it was *real* tobacco: strong and free of the 7,000 chemicals, 70 of which are carcinogens, added to American cigarettes.[2] She could walk to class carrying a stack of books in one hand and pack and roll a cigarette with the other—in the wind. I saw her do it. We would sit on the floor of our dorm, for hours, talking about the world.

Dorm life with sun and European tobacco

---

[2] American Cancer Society

When my year of classes was done and I was working in Boston, I was hooked again but never fell completely back in. I'd buy a pack of cigarettes every morning on the way to work, smoke two, and throw the pack away. Buy a pack on the way home, smoke two, throw it away. Next morning, same thing. On the way back from visiting a friend in Dedham, only a thirty-minute drive, I'd do the same thing. A gigantic waste of money. But I'd had enough years of knowing freedom, and looking back, I have affectionate feelings for how hard I was trying to fight it off. When I moved back to Milwaukee in 1997, I finally left them behind for good.

To demonstrate again how insidious cigarette addiction is, for ten years after I quit, even though I never thought about smoking, I had many dreams about having "just one cigarette without worrying about being hooked." Eventually, I was free from the dreams too.

CHAPTER 3

Alcohol

I also drank in excess. My mom and dad (and brothers and sister for that matter) didn't drink. When I was seven or eight, I went with my dad to a church dinner. Someone offered him a beer. "No, I'd better not. I'm driving," he said. Our church was ten blocks away. In later years, he kept a case of warm Blatz and Michelob in his basement workshop. When a certain mailman came by, he'd offer him a beer, and they'd sit and chat. I'm not sure why the mailman accepted booze on the job, but considering my dad was offering warm beer, God bless him for being gracious. He must have enjoyed visiting with my dad to accept the lukewarm offerings. When I look back, how I'd love to know what they talked about and wish I'd listened instead of going to my room to blare *Zeppelin IV* or *Million Dollar Babies*. I only saw my mom have a drink once when we were visiting friends, and it was the only time in my whole life I saw her giggle. It made her look like a young girl. It was beautiful to see. (The drink was, of course, a Tom Collins.) It made me see my mom and dad for the first time as young people in love instead of as a mom and dad cleaning windows, taking out the trash, and trying to get a closet door back on its track.

Like many people, I'm sure, my drinking started at high school parties. I was a pretty social person and don't think I leaned on alcohol to ward off awkwardness. I guess it was just what everyone was doing. But I always got really drunk. To this day, I have a hard time hiding the effect of even one glass of wine. I've never understood how it's supposed to be all right for people to drink but not all right to show it's affecting them.

High school parties were just the warm-up. There were nights when I had eight or nine T&T's. And at the "obligatory" Milwaukee Friday fish fry, four or five or even six Southern Comfort Old-Fashioneds. I had to work one Saturday morning after drinking all night and got home so late, I didn't bother going to bed. I went right into work, wearing the same clothes, probably still drunk. In Colorado, a guy called me after a night out, and I didn't know who he was. There was a work party when I had a couple shots of vodka before I even left, drank all night, and ran off the driveway when I started home. (They made me come back inside to sober up.) Once, I was out drinking in Appleton and ran into a ditch; the people in a house next door pushed me out. (I went back the next day to thank them. Pathetic.) There was the night in Chicago with friends when I drank so much, I didn't recognize the photos we took. I was so sick the next day and crammed into a tiny elevator headed to the top of the Sears tower. (I'm still not sure how I got through that.) Oh, and that time I fell off a pier at 2 a.m. in northern Wisconsin.

I was aware of the problem, skipping a temp job Christmas work party in the early eighties, knowing I'd end up drinking too much. I wasn't in a personal place to abstain, but at least I had enough sense to decline the invite. In the mid-eighties, three of my friends threw an intervention: "We all met to go bowling, but after one beer, all you wanted to do was drink." I wish I could say this was a seminal moment, but I hadn't yet done the deep reflective work necessary to change. Looking back, I appreciate the courage it must have taken for my friends to break the fun of our youthful exuberance for something so important.

Aside from all the terrifying things that could have happened from my actions—and thankfully didn't by the grace of God and/or blind luck—it makes me sad to consider all the precious days in my one precious life that were wasted on suffering and recovering.

Even given all the horribleness, I'm still not sure if I was or am an alcoholic because, in my early fifties, after I'd decided I no longer wanted to throw away my sacred time on this Earth, I was able to stop. And although I know aging metabolism plays a part, stopping was effortless. Again, just a decision. Since 2016 or so, I rarely have more than one glass of wine at dinner, if that. As tempting as a second glass might be, I'm always able to channel my dad and say, "No, I'd better not."

The abuse was probably more about my excess habit. I've never sipped wine or beer slowly, savoring and enjoying, unless I'm in a setting where I have to adhere to social protocol so I don't look like a cretin. That makes me think I drank for the initial buzz. Kind of like the first hit of pot.

CHAPTER 4

Pot

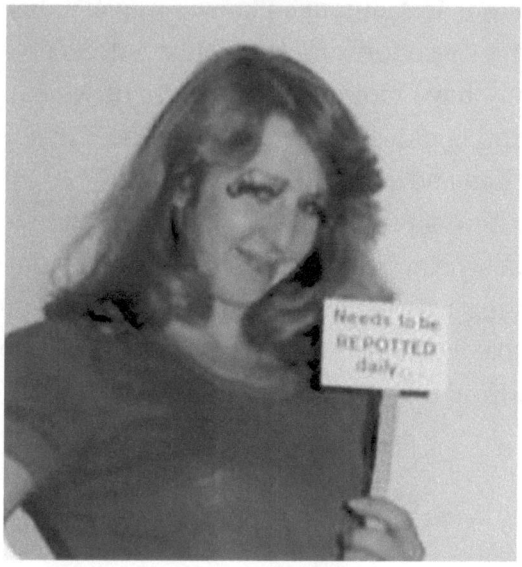

Working on our Plant Halloween costumes—
with Tanqueray in our watering cans

I smoked a lot of pot. A *lot*. I understand that to some people, the thought of using drugs is abhorrent. When I was caught up in the flurry of being a teenager, I saw an interview on *60 Minutes* with Bill Russell. I wasn't interested in basketball, so I have no idea what made me watch. Perhaps his distinctive voice. When asked if he'd ever used drugs, he said something I've never forgotten: "No, I guess I always just wanted to live life at its *own pace*." I loved how he said it. Writing this at sixty-five,

I now understand that the most precious experience anyone can have in their life is to live it naturally: the joys and sorrows, the exciting and routine. (Ask a Holocaust survivor if any day is routine.) But back then, I was definitely not Bill Russell.

I've tried to estimate how much pot I smoked between 1976 (when I had my first hit off a joint inside the auditorium at a David Bowie concert) and 2005 (when I finished off four odds and ends bags from friends who'd moved). An ounce lasted about a month, and I smoked mostly between 1982 and 2000. So maybe around 144 ounces? That's probably a little high (pun definitely intended), but I smoked *a lot* of pot. I don't want to even think about how much money might be in my bank account now instead of up in smoke (and *another*). My ability to clean an ounce on an album cover rivaled the skill of any old-world European artisan. My (appropriated) personal motto: "No flake left behind."

I tried other things. I had some pretty blue mescaline powder with a girlfriend in the van of some guys we didn't know at the Pink Floyd *Dark Side of the Moon* concert—the one where they kept playing during a thunderstorm and David Gilmour ad-libbed, "When I'm cold and tired—and wet." I smoked mushrooms with a friend and went to Target to buy the game Trouble with our hair in mini pigtails (not sure what that was), laughing hysterically in the aisles. I popped a good number of White Cross—so many around, they practically spilled out of our high school lockers. I swear this is true: During a Jefferson Starship concert, I looked down at my hands, and they looked fuzzy and orange and felt fuzzy too. I bought hash at a high school dance. I dipped cigarettes in hash oil—actually, that's worth trying once (*ha ha*). I tried coke just once. It was the eighties, and what you hear about cocaine is true: All of a sudden, *I knew everything and had the answer to life*—and I proceeded to tell everyone else (for hours). Thankfully, something instinctual warned me not to do that again, and I didn't. I was probably able to draw that "line" (another irresistible pun) because I preferred the comfy, dozy feeling of getting high to the crazy of coke.

Pot was the best. There was nothing better than getting high in the morning. I recognize the paradox: We put something damaging into our physical body in the morning, but it is, in fact, the magic of our physical body's daily rejuvenation that makes the morning abuse possible. Pot in the morning shifts time more profoundly than Thomas Mann's *The Magic Mountain*. When straight, I'd plan and allocate my couple of hours before work; when I had pot, if I had just five minutes (*plenty of time!*), I'd take a hit, lay back, and float through each languid one.

I could write for hours about how much and how flagrantly I toked, but here are two good examples. Once, I smoked so much when I was living with three girls in Boston that I fell to the ground, hearing an electrical zap in my brain, but got up to smoke more. I also got high *two hours before having shoulder surgery!* I swear this is true: The music piped into the operating room before I went under was "Last Dance With Mary Jane."

The craziness of the above notwithstanding, there were highs (can't stop!) to smoking: going somewhere with friends and yelling out of the car window with joy, "I love life! I love being alive!"; making cookies that looked like penises with my girlfriend and laughing so hard we were crying; listening to *The Best of ABBA* while stoned (also actually worth trying); and looking at some mundane thing and suddenly seeing it completely differently.

But there were also lows: the feeling I got, like any addict, when I was almost out; the anxious high instead of the relaxed high that came with being almost out; scraping the pipe screen and bottom of the pot storage canister to scratch together *just one more bowl* (including getting on hands and knees to look for tiny pieces that might have fallen on the floor—God only knows what else was added from the floor to the mix); smoking so much that my throat hurt and I was continually coughing; feeling a dark cloud come over me when I was finally out and had to go "back to normal life" until I got the next ounce.

If I'd been old enough for Woodstock, I definitely would have been one of the people passed out in the medical tent instead of enjoying the music. I finally did circle back to joining Mr. Russell in living life at its own magnificent pace. Thank you, Bill.

CHAPTER 5

Shoulders

Spontaneous backflip on Daytona Beach

My drive to excess took the greatest toll on my shoulders, leading to five surgeries: 1997 right cartilage repair, 2000 second right repair, 2009 third right repair, 2010 right replacement, and 2011 left repair. I know exactly how I ruined them: backbends.

Like most teenagers, I had a lot of pent-up energy, and my mom would tell me to go run around the block. Instead of sounding like an excellent idea (which, of course, it was), it sounded like the boring thing a parent says. Instead of heeding the advice, I'd go into my room, put on loud music, and do backbends. Lots and lots of backbends. And I didn't just bend over backward. I had a super flexible spine, and I'd fling myself back, reaching the ground in an instant, stand up, fly back again, and stand up—over and over. At school, in the hallway, someone would say, "Kathy, do the backbend thing!" and I'd drop my books and fly back into one. And every time I did it (without any stretching or warm-up), my shoulder ligaments became more and more stretched out. The stage had been set.

After high school, I moved nine times between 1977 and 1997, carting everything myself except for the couch and a heavy dresser. All other large pieces of furniture were taken up and down stairs and around corners by me. I lugged an ancient heavy air conditioner and a heavy six-drawer wooden cabinet up three flights of stairs. I still don't know how, but I think I know why: the curse of the Prussian work ethic inherited from my maternal grandmother's side. *I can do it myself!*

Between 1985 and 1993, I lived in a four-apartment building. It was beautiful and three blocks from the neighborhood library. *Heaven.* Looking to save money on rent, I cut the lawn and shoveled snow. I actually enjoyed doing those things—seeing the neat tracks of cut grass as I mowed and finishing the edges of snow on each side of the walk just so, like my dad's extra attention to detail in everything he did.

I worked 3 p.m. to 11 p.m. for many years and spent wonderful summer afternoons in the sun, cutting, trimming, and watering the grass. There's something satisfying about watering grass. After work on balmy summer evenings at my childhood home, a city house with a postage-stamp-sized front and backyard, my dad would sit in a lawn chair and water, relaxing and greeting passersby. Taking care of the apartment's lawn gave me that same sense of satisfaction, but it also added more stress to already stressed shoulders.

Shoveling snow was the hardest. There used to be a hell of a lot more snow during Midwestern winters. It seemed like I was out there every day, clearing the front and back walks, stairs, and parking area. I'd do a round before I left for work at 3 p.m. and another after I got home at 11. Even shoveling snow, like watering in summer, can be magical—being out in the raw elements and frigid air, with stars sparkling overhead—unless it was deep, wet, and heavy as lead, trodden down by foot traffic. My shoulders continued to break down.

FIRST DISLOCATION

When Shoulder Dislocation Day came in October 1994, my thirty-six-year-old abused shoulder was practically begging to be wrenched from its socket. It was my second month of graduate school in Boston, and I was taking a shower and fretting over a paper. I guess anxiety fueled blind determination because, when I stepped out, I forcefully flung the shower curtain open in a wide sweeping motion. Out came the shoulder bone, *wedging behind the socket.* I didn't even realize what had happened—I just stared at it, perplexed. The natural round bump where my shoulder should have been was indented and concave, and my arm stuck out to the back. It didn't hurt because the nerves were temporarily deadened. I called campus security and was rushed to the hospital.

A nurse observed that when shoulders dislocate, they fall to the front. She'd never seen one wedged behind the socket. I lay there with my arm hanging off the table for about an hour, waiting for the specialist, shaking from nervousness, trying to imagine how one even puts a shoulder bone back in. Nervousness turned to fear during discussions of whether they could put me under because I'd eaten breakfast. There was great relief when they decided it had been long enough and they could. I woke up with my arm bandaged to my side and the nerves coming alive.

As I write this thirty years later, I can still feel the pain.

Unbelievably, I was in class the next day, arm banded against my body, lugging heavy books with my other hand. I guess I didn't have a choice. I couldn't sit in my dorm, missing classes and falling behind just as I was starting the semester.

That fall consisted of cold, dark, dreary New England days spent in pain: going to class during the day, grocery shopping and doing laundry one-handed at night (transported there by bus because I couldn't drive my stick), and returning home to the cement dorm room that was never quite warm enough and a hard bed. I can't imagine how I managed it all. But it's always that way—you do what you have to.

There was no psychological stress to burden me. I was a pure pragmatic reaction machine only. I hadn't fully comprehended what had happened—the trauma to my body, the damage to bone, the wrenching of the muscles and nerves, the need for physical, emotional, and psychic self-care. A friend once observed that any cut into the body is traumatizing, and I understand that now. But back then, I was clueless about the enormity of what had happened. At my office manager job seven months later, I was carrying boxes of copy paper from the store to the office (in the prehistoric age before Amazon). For $25, I could have at least purchased a handcart, but doing something like that never occurred to me. My shoulder had come out and been put back in, and I thought that would be the end of it. Until I was just walking down the stairs one day, swinging my arms, and felt it stick again.

Little did I know, my shoulders would dominate my life for the next twenty years: five surgeries; tens of thousands of dollars in medical bills; a middle-of-the-night ER visit in my pajamas, where I waited four hours with another dislocation, watching gunshot wounds (understandably) get taken before me; 183 PT sessions (to my best count), many during winter, where I managed to get myself dressed with one hand and waited for buses in the freezing cold; five two-month absences from work; lost days when I was so scared to move my arm, I slept with it tied to my side. And continual discomfort and pain and worry.

SURGERY #1

Around the time I'd decided to leave the personal injury law firm out east, my mom had a car accident.[3] During my mom's post-accident medical care, dementia was diagnosed. Wanting to keep her in her home, I (happily) arrived back in October 1996 to live with her. Two months later I was startled awake, feeling like my right shoulder wasn't completely in the socket. I'd have to have surgery, a repair to shredded labrum, the cartilage that helps hold joints in place. Four things doomed that surgery.

First, just days after, I was up again, carrying the laundry downstairs and doing other household chores. I felt prickles in my shoulder but still didn't have enough sense to take it easy. *That Prussian curse?* It was probably more about feeling like I was playing the role of "caretaker." These things *had to be done*. But I was pulling and tearing the sutures.

Second, I wasn't working, didn't have health insurance for physical therapy, and the surgeon agreed that swimming could be a good way to strengthen the shoulder. So I hit the pool but, as usual, went overboard (can't stop the puns). I didn't try to pace myself, tried to do lap turns like an athlete, and all without any warm-up. Probably more damage than PT.

Third, my family home was in a flood-prone area at the

---

[3] Fortune had been with her: it was one block from her house, and the neighbors whose mailbox was damaged were kind. She voluntarily relinquished her license. As difficult a decision as this is for anyone, it must have been especially hard for her. Her father taught her to drive, and one of her first jobs was delivering cars for a company that sold them. Throughout my life, she always took long drives in the surrounding Milwaukee area. Whenever she wasn't around, we knew she was on a drive. I admire her for loving it so much yet so wisely and voluntarily giving it up.

bottom of a hill. We had one soon after my surgery. Three feet of water in the basement, and everything downstairs had to go. There I was again, before being healed, lifting and hauling.

Fourth, because of the flooding, we had to have the basement reinforced. The house had a side walkway made of large stones with space in between. The contractor left the stones coated with a thick, spongy mud that had to be cleaned. I used a narrow, sharp shovel and began scraping—for hours. The task was grueling, and I was pounding the tool on the hard stone out of pure frustration. I can still feel the sharp pain in my shoulder bones—*that I never thought to shield myself from*. I must have been desperately trying to tell myself something that I wasn't hearing. It certainly wasn't the message of self-care.

SURGERY #2

In 1999 I was working as the office manager at a large agency. Because of general neglect in past years, the overhead lights were filled with dead flies. Not sure what the catalyst was for cleaning them (I probably said something because I couldn't stand it), but instead of suggesting that outside help be brought in, I volunteered to take care of them. I spent an entire Saturday placing a ladder under each light, reaching up to remove the sheet, cleaning it, and reaching up to put it back into place—a job for two or three people. I could barely feel my shoulders when I was done. More abuse on a never-healed shoulder.

It all caught up with me by 2000 when my shoulder partially dislocated again. Back for a second repair. I wasn't offered mechanical tools, but at least I had health insurance for PT.

Only after experiencing quality PT from later surgeries did I realize those first sessions weren't what they should have been: do ten of these, do ten of those, no attention to form, see you next time. And although the state of my shoulder was starting to get my attention, I still wasn't in a mental place to take more control of my recovery.

SURGERY #3

In 2001, I was at an agency that contracted with a state social service organization. State file reviews meant lugging boxes (sometimes twenty to thirty)—in the days before electronic records—to the bureau and picking them up again. When we expanded to sixty case managers, we had two weeks to prepare the office desks vacated by the none-too-happy former workers who'd left a mess. I was new, there was a task to be done, and I offered to do it. I bought two large McDonald's coffees (another bad habit I would eventually break) and spent an entire Saturday cleaning old, sticky, God knows what and scrubbing, moving, lifting, and clearing sixty desks and work areas. It never occurred to me to ask for help.

It all caught up with me once more in 2006. I'd been sleeping with my right arm stretched over my head and woke with a start. Out of the socket again. It was the middle of the night, so I called an ambulance. I managed to get into jeans (with my pajama top—and no bra. The horror!) and landed in the ER. It was a busy night, and I sat there for almost four hours as they triaged gunshot wounds and stabbings (unfortunately, I'm not exaggerating). I was finally seen around 4 a.m. when a physician assistant trainee, under the guidance of another PA, was going to put my arm back in while I was awake. They put me on my stomach, where I lay shaking. It actually wasn't as terrible as I'd thought, but, like always, the pain arrives when the nerves revive. More pain pills (pre-opioid crisis), slapped a smiley face on my sling, and at work the next day.

The years 2006 and 2007 were bad. I was scared to do anything—even drying myself off with a towel after a shower was frightening. I slept with my right arm tied around my waist to keep it from coming out during the night.

Despite my caution, the shoulder almost dislocated again in 2008. The surgeon I'd been seeing on the outskirts of Milwaukee had referred me to a more veteran colleague. I figured I might as well go to someone closer and found a prominent, caring surgeon. He was going to have his hands full with my shoulder. After recounting my history and declaring that I needed a new one, he replied that because I was "only" fifty-three, he was confident a repair would suffice. I might have imagined it, but I believe, after the surgery, he said I had the shoulder of an eighty-year-old. Replacement surgery was scheduled for 2009. Until then, it was two more months off work, pain, money, and PT. But this time, everything was done right: mechanical PT machine and large cold pack contraption that was nearly impossible to get on alone—kind of like wrestling an alligator. (I've never wrestled an alligator.)

In another stroke of luck, I found Southern Lakes Physical Therapy (now called Thera Dynamics Physical Therapy), owned by Bill Lois. SLPT's care was high quality, especially in comparison to my former places (where a therapist literally left the building with me still lying on the table).

But SLPT's therapy was an art: a combination of expertise, undivided attention, encouragement, and humor.

SURGERY #4

Unlike the first few times, I knew I'd need help after the shoulder replacement surgery, so my sister and sister-in-law each spent two weeks with me. I cannot thank them enough.[4]

I hated the weekly Coumadin blood draws that hurt more each time, and I can't imagine how people with heart conditions bear getting checked routinely. My hand blew up to the size of an orange (a crazy feeling), and I had lymph therapy to manually massage and move the blocked channels. It made me aware of my mysterious lymphatic system, and I still brush my skin. If I had nine lives, I'd spend one as a lymphatic therapist.

SURGERY #5

Seven months after my replacement, I noticed my left shoulder sticking. I hadn't had problems on that side, but, given my history, I had it checked. There were tears—two more months off work, more pain, more PT, more money.

Titanium replacements last about twenty years. No problem if you're eighty when you get one. A bigger one if you're fifty-three. Some people have goals of traveling the world or buying a home on a lake. My life goal is to keep my shoulders in their sockets.

---

[4] Going through surgery takes a lot of preparation, especially when you're single, and my tip sheet is attached.

CHAPTER 6

Jaw

My right jaw is slightly misaligned. It sounds worse than it is and actually doesn't bother me that much. I suspect that my crazy flying backbends had something to do with that too. Like most of our asymmetrical bodies, the left side of my body has always been better than the right: left foot a half-size bigger, left thumb noticeably larger, larger left breast (really), and left profile better than the right. So it's not surprising that my right shoulder and right jaw folded more easily under the abuse.

I mention it all to illustrate how strong yet potentially fragile our skeletons are. I was used to seeing them at Halloween or hanging in science rooms, but I never saw them as the fascinating, connected assembly of ligaments and tendons and muscles that they are. Lugging around a twenty-pound purse into your seventies will constantly pull one side of your skeleton. Just like a teenager with too much energy, whipping herself into backbends (2,000 over the years?) will cause damage.

PART II

EARLY FITNESS ATTEMPTS

I'd always been pretty active, which made how bad I felt surprising. Early activities at the seventies' exercise chain Elaine Powers instilled me with a useful lifelong tool. The others only added to the damage.

I didn't like my body as a teenager, and my unhappiness must have been evident because, bless her heart, my mom signed me up in high school at Elaine Powers where I could walk after classes. It surprises me that I wasn't embarrassed going there—any socially conscious teenager would be—especially given it was along my friends' path home. Going to Elaine Powers seemed like having a key to a grown-up place in a grown-up world.

When you went in, you retrieved your workout card with your exercise plan, checking off items as you worked through them. It was probably better than doing nothing, but two of the machines were the roller thing you placed your legs or butt against and just stood there and a vibrating belt to put around your midsection—vital organ freak-out. There were some real leg lifts and probably other things too. Routine content notwithstanding, Elaine Powers gave me something that stuck: Retrieving my card with a set plan and methodically filling in the boxes gave me a valuable model I'd often use in the future—exercise tools.

CHAPTER 7

Exercise Tools

I made *a lot* of these in the early years, handwritten, using rulers on legal-size paper in the Stone Age before computers. My mom said she could always tell when I was making some kind of chart because she'd hear the ruler dropping on my desk at regular intervals.

	May 1	May 2	May 3	May 4	May 5
10 arms					
10 sit-ups					
10 leg lifts					
10 back kicks					
10 twists					
10 jacks					

Like the cards, the tools made things structured and easy. The only thing I had to do before going to bed each night was make sure there was a checkmark in every box. Over thirty years, I made many other charts: drink more water, take vitamins, meditate, etc.

But the charts had problems: I wasn't necessarily doing the best things or doing them correctly, they lasted only until my columns ran out and weren't continued, and I wasn't doing anything to change other harmful habits.

So ingrained was the concept of exercise tools that they stayed with me even during one of my most egregiously unhealthy periods. I lived with a couple in northern Wisconsin. The wife drank ten Cokes a day (I saw it), and the husband had a good job and was a hard worker but drank beer from the time he got home until he went to bed. They even had a keg inside a second refrigerator in their kitchen. I drank a lot of that beer. It's painful and embarrassing to think about throwing up once in the wastebasket in my room. But even in the middle of all that unhealthiness, and I can't recall how long I kept it up, I still did those damn exercises: front leg lifts, back leg lifts, side leg lifts. They probably had no effect at all because I did them in starts and stops, with no warm-up—and probably while drunk. But the Elaine Powers discipline stayed with me, somewhere deep down, to be revived many years later. Thank you, Mom. Thank you, Elaine.

CHAPTER 8

Health Clubs

The year after high school graduation, in 1978, a friend and I signed up at the new Vic Tanny, a subterranean women-only fitness club. And I mean subterranean. You walked in and headed down a dark, narrow, orange shag-carpeted hallway to stairs leading into a basement with small offices and one large workout room. It was new then, but I wouldn't want to think about the smell of all that accumulated sweat over time. The representative met with us and noted that I indeed had some weight to lose. We did wonder, however, when she said the same thing to my tall, lean friend. We chalked it up to the business pitch.

Everything was about weight instead of fitness in those days. I don't remember much about what we did (there were some group classes), but the club paved the way for my 1982 membership with the very new and very improved Vic Tanny. In only three years, the underground fortress had evolved into a real gym: suburban location, floor-to-ceiling windows all around, two floors, full array of machines, pool, and a huge room with floor-to-ceiling mirrors for the new *aerobics* craze.

That 1982 Vic Tanny membership cost $600 up front for two years, with a 2.5 percent increase every year. The contract was the legal-size thing you sign to buy a car.[5]

It was indeed the eighties, and I went all in with a black leotard, black tights, colorful polyester-sheen half top that served no purpose, and—yes—leg warmer socks. What Madison Avenue advertising magician got people to believe those were necessary?

Ridiculous as we looked, it was the first place I did some real aerobics and lower body machine exercise. But even though I looked the part, I still wasn't getting it. For some weird reason, I felt I needed to "fuel up" before going to aerobics, and my go-to was pancakes with syrup (don't ask me). I was trying, but I just didn't have the knowledge and tools to do things the right way.

Another friend and I joined a local health club in the mid-1980s. We did some machines but mostly sat in the sauna and always stopped at the Taco Bell next door after. Any workout benefits were smothered in taco sauce.

I'd fallen in love with aerobics at Vic Tanny, and, in the second half of the '80s, I took many community classes at area schools. I was still working second shift and got home around 11, but I was always at my place, on the floor, by 6 a.m. to dance—oops, I mean exercise. I'd always dreamed about being part of a dance troupe, and I guess these classes satisfied that desire. But again, as always, it was all done with no warm-up, all while hopping from bar to bar, joint to joint—and always accompanied by junk food.

---

[5] I paid the fee every year faithfully, even while I went away to school in Boston. I shared with others how "reasonable" the yearly increase was and how keeping it active since 1982, even during the fifteen-year period of my shoulder surgeries, was one of the smartest things I ever did. Only after Blast (Vic Tanny/Bally/Blast ownership) went out of business in 2019 did I discover that a basic Planet Fitness membership is $10 a month. That myopic vision taught me it always pays to look around and see what other options are out there.

CHAPTER 9

Tennis

Nan Gilbert's *Champions Don't Cry*[6] captured my teenage heart. Enough so that I asked my mom to take a photo of me leaning on our garage door, holding my tennis racket and a sign I'd made saying, "Champions don't cry"—while pretending to cry (?). I spent a lot of time slamming tennis balls against that uneven door, watching them ricochet left and right. It must have made my parents insane, and I thank them for letting me do it.

Fifteen years later, I took lessons at my old high school. I loved tennis, the precision of the swing (*swing like you're wiping off the top of a table*), racing to the right spot, stopping, solidly planting yourself for the swing, the feel of the ball hitting and leaving the racket's sweet spot.

I spent many afternoons playing with a friend at a local park and was in a women's league for a short while. I had to play doubles with a very pregnant partner and was crazy with worry the whole time that I'd hit her. I loved singles—detested doubles.

I was also in a city tournament. I wasn't a practiced player and still marvel that I had the gumption to sign up. I won the morning match and advanced to another in the afternoon. But to show how clueless I was, instead of doing something productive and healthy in between, I had a huge fish fry lunch. Needless

---

[6]   Nan Gilbert, *Champions Don't Cry* (Harper & Brothers 1960).

to say, the sluggish person who hit the court in the afternoon (plus three pounds of carbs and salt) was not the warrior of the morning. I lost.

And again, during all of the tennis, no warm-up, no cool down. My swings got better and better, but my shoulders got worse and worse.

CHAPTER 10

Swimming

Heaven

My favorite thing is to be in water. Returning to the embryonic sac? I often dream I'm in water at our central Wisconsin cottage—but more like a fish than a person, flipping over and around, in and out, gravity-free, light as air. I spent hours swimming in that lake until the sun set. Sunset was the best, air cooling, making the water feel even warmer.

But for some reason, I hated my fourth-grade swimming lessons. Maybe it was the damp, musty chlorine smell. Or being forced to hold my breath, or gasping for breath. I felt trapped and scared there. In hindsight, holding onto a pool ledge, gently kicking, and moving my head to the side is pretty easy, but I guess nothing is easy in the fourth grade.

My mom, fifty-five at the time, said, "If you walk out of the lesson with a smile, I'll ride bikes with you." I summoned a smile and chose the steep hill in front of our house. What a little shit. I can still see her struggling to get to the top. After those lessons, I didn't swim for thirty years.

I rediscovered and learned to love the pool in the mid-2000s. It had been a few years since my second surgery, and I thought my shoulders were "back to normal." I spent hours in that pool, morning sun spilling through the windows.

CHAPTER 11

Skating

I loved ice-skating. My cousin lived on a lake, and her dad would clear smooth, winding paths through the snow on the frozen water. Skating on the paths was fun enough during the day, but it was especially wonderful at night with the lights of the house radiating a warm glow onto the ice. How delicious to skate until you couldn't feel your nose and then head into the brightly lit house for hot chocolate. I was fortunate to have had skating lessons. (More thanks, Mom.) I only took them for a year, but it was long enough to feel the satisfaction of making controlled, perfect figure-eight edges and skating backward fast enough to imagine I was in the Olympics.

I also always liked roller-skating and going to our high school roller-skating dances—although, naturally, most of the time was spent looking at boys. When I left a job in 2012 and had time during the day, I went into the roller rink near my house. The rink was filled with around thirty senior citizens at 10 a.m. I picked out my skates from the rink's supply (can't imagine doing that now... yuck!) and wobbled onto the track. First time around was a little shaky, but soon I was smoothly rolling even though it had been forty years. And I felt confident enough to enjoy turning by crossing a leg in front and looking around.

I witnessed a very beautiful thing: these seniors, whose

age took its toll when walking, were transformed into flowing angels on skates. Gliding smoothly, seamlessly, smiling. It was a scene I will never forget, and I went back several times. The rink closed in August 2022, and only after I saw articles about it did I realize what a community treasure it had been. The older folks I'd had the joy of watching had probably been going there since they were young and must have felt very sad to have their skating and community time end.

In 2019, I bought used rollerblades at a rummage sale. A friend gently suggested I also take the elbow and knee pads. That hadn't even occurred to me, still nine years old in my head, and I scoffed. Then I remembered I was sixty-one and grabbed the padding too. I held off on the helmet—just wouldn't fit with my vision of the wind in my hair as I skated away on my river of happiness. I found a large, smooth school parking lot and went crazy. You'd think I was trying to out-skate Beth Heiden: leaning low, pushing off hard, tight turns. Kathy Bauernfeind, Olympic Rollerblading Phenomenon. I skated for over an hour. Felt great driving home. Half an hour later, I lost control of how my feet hit the floor—with dead flops like Frankenstein. My excess mentality had overdone it again. So long skating.

CHAPTER 12

Belly Dancing

By 2007, I could no longer swim or play tennis or get too crazy in aerobics class, so I signed up for belly dancing, thinking it would be a good way to get some exercise within my shoulder limitations. It started out okay, and I picked up the basics, but I soon realized there's still a lot of arms in belly dancing—and mine just couldn't do it. When we did a circle thing with everyone getting a turn in the middle, people were getting better, I was stuck on the basics, and the fun drained away. But wearing that thing with the little bangles around my waist and the finger cymbals was damn fun.

CHAPTER 13

Fred Astaire

I got involved with Fred Astaire in the early eighties after a coworker invited me to one of her shows. It was probably another opportunity to feel like a professional dancer, if not quite the *Jesus Christ Superstar* Simon Zealot running across the desert scene. Or maybe it was just the sparkly costumes. I spent six months and lots of money being glided around the floor by suave instructors. At the time, I thought the "rich old ladies" in the shows, who were basically getting lifted up and carried around by male dancers, were kind of foolish. Now that I'm closer to their age, I think, *Goddamn, good for them for getting out of their chairs and living*. Another lesson I've never forgotten. I enjoyed the dancing, but it was more loosening up of already loose shoulders.

I spent the first fifty-five years of my life a victim of excess and self-abuse. Despite a wide array of activities, none done correctly, my body was broken. I was overweight, my muscles hurt, my joints cracked, and my energy was gone. I thought it was inevitable—that I was just getting old and that my best days were behind me. I was miserable and desperate.

PART III

PREPARING FOR RECOVERY

It was probably the desperation and seeing older, active, healthy people (*They must be exceptions and were probably healthy their whole lives*, I thought), but I started to wonder if I could save myself, if feeling lousy as I aged wasn't inevitable like we're conditioned to believe ("it's all downhill after forty"). I started to wonder if I still had time. After all, I figured, it might not be too late to at least do *something*.[7]

---

[7] I came to learn that being older can actually be a benefit when you're trying to get healthy. It's easier to stay focused. Your improved focus helps you recognize the changes. And you understand the stakes.

CHAPTER 14

Reasons to Fight Back

Smiling but aching

Something deep down was making me want to fight back. Looking back, I can see it was a combination of five things.

FEELING LOUSY

I was caught in the old trap: getting home from work, having dinner, dozing off in a chair, and rousing myself enough to wash my face, brush my teeth, and go to bed. One winter, I had the idea that I should run into the frigid air near the end of the evenings to slap some life into myself. But I was too lazy to even do that. I was working at an extremely stressful, energy-draining job. But there were also the aches and pains. My body hurt.

I was starting to feel old and wasn't enjoying my life. I'd left a job but worried I wouldn't have the physical and mental energy to start a new one. Funny, since I was the girl who spent hours jumping Double Dutch and running around the neighborhood until I dropped. In 2017, I walked a couple miles in the Komen Race for the Cure, and my hip hurt. Just from walking.[8]

I also started thinking about my heart. In the late 1960s, I was under the spell of the Monkees and of course started a fan club with three other girls, each of us taking one of the guys. I liked Peter but had to be Davy because I could do an English accent. Jones dying of a heart attack in 2012 shook me. As I would begin moving and exercising in a coordinated and healthy way in the coming years, I thought often about how strong it was making my heart. The heart is actually pretty small, and it scared me to think about how hard I was making it pump. But I knew it was good for me.

My body was hanging on. But the question for me was whether hanging on was good enough. At the crossroads of significantly changing what they eat and how they move, some

---

[8] A Double Dutch parable: I spent hours and hours jumping in my diverse childhood neighborhood. Nimble, light as a feather, on one foot, double time, bending down and touching the ground, turning around, in and out through the ropes. I liked turning too—the feeling of the long ropes gently and rhythmically moving my body to the left, then right. I stopped jumping when we moved and didn't think about it until years later when I was telling a coworker how much I'd loved it. Her nieces still jumped and, to my indescribable delight, I was asked to join. I immediately began to wonder if I'd still have the energy thirty-six years later. I was up, they began turning, and all of a sudden, I stopped cold, realizing I'd completely forgotten *how to do it*! I tried a few times, but when I heard "next," I knew my dreams of jumping were over. This sad saga contains a profound lesson. I'd been so focused on being "too old" that I never thought about the "how."

people might feel that hanging on is good enough. But that wasn't how I wanted to "be" in the world. I was tired of feeling tired. And I realized there was no time to mess around (I used a different word in my journal).

FEAR OF DEATH

The reality that we're going to die seems to sink in around midlife for most, but it found me at six. My brother was playing a song that had a tolling bell. I thought it was Tom Lehrer but have never been able to find it in his collections. Whether it was the lyrics or the bell, I knew that song was about death. And not funny death like at the *Monty Python's The Meaning of Life* dinner party where they all die from the salmon mousse (in which Michael Palin was—well, no superlatives suffice). Whatever that song was, death might as well have been standing next to me in the living room because, in that moment, I understood that one day I was going to die. I can clearly remember, as if it were happening right now, walking into the kitchen and telling my mom that I, at six, didn't want to die. The memory ends there, but I can only imagine what her reaction must have been!

I'm guessing many people don't want to die because they're afraid of how it will happen. Or because they don't know what comes after. Or they fear being forgotten. Or they haven't lived to their fullest potential. Or they'll die before they've contributed something to the world. Or they'll miss their loved ones. My fear was that I was simply going to miss being in the world. What Robert Frost called the "materiality" (not materialism) of life.

Despite my precocious confrontation with death, I didn't dwell on it. But a subtle anxiety was there, for about forty-five years, until I had an epiphany that brought me peace.

I lived a few blocks from the St. Francis Seminary on the Milwaukee lakefront and spent more hours than I could count walking there: deer at dusk, fox in the dewy mornings, birds, squirrels—the grounds alive with nature. Filled with stately trees: deep green in spring and summer, blanketed with snow in winter, and brilliantly yellow, orange, and red in fall. I was walking on a warm, glorious fall day, and in the middle of a sea of golden trees, I stopped short. I still don't know where it came from, but right then, I understood that my body was made of the same golden leaves on the trees—new buds flittering in the gentlest of breezes, young, robust, strong green leaves, then growing brittle, then gone. Trees go through the cycle in a year. Our cycles are longer but the same. Instead of feeling sad about dying, I understood and accepted the process. It was sacred, and I was honored to be part of it.

The day I realized my place in this world

That understanding of the cycle of life related to my desire to fight for my health. If I'm part of the natural world, I want to be in it as I'd been made to be in it, without all the bad things I'd been putting into, and doing to, my body. Death would be inevitable, but I didn't want mine to be because of something I did or didn't do to care for the golden tree that is my body.

GETTING OLD

Making my artificial shoulder strong for the future was important, but envisioning my future health was even more so. I asked myself, *How do I want to be in this world? How will I want to be in this world as I age? What will it feel like to be eighty-five?*

When I was growing up in the sixties and seventies, old people looked really old: feeble, bent over, in wheelchairs, or stationary. I wanted to spend the last part of my life standing up instead of worrying about falling down. I wanted strong bones and muscles so that if I did fall, I could get back up![9]

As bleak as my models of old age were, two things in my head fought them and helped me move forward. The first were those people I'd seen in their seventies and eighties who still looked great and were working out, running, and doing sports. The second was the memory of my nine-year-old's energy still alive inside me. I've always lived in three worlds: remembering what it felt like to be young, being able to view things from the perspective of me as a very old woman (God willing), and feeling where I currently am. It was an admittedly tall order to imagine I could still run around outside, full speed, for hours, but I also knew I was many years away from being inside a body that couldn't move at all.

These were still the early days when I didn't yet understand how much power I had to change how I'd feel when I got old. I just knew I was still too far away from those days to feel like I was already feeling. I instinctively knew that feeling old wasn't inevitable, and I was determined to control it.

Feeling lousy, fear of death, and fear of getting old all led me to ask myself one question: *Do I want things to be different?* The answer was yes. I wanted to feel excited about who I was. I wanted to be a "winner." And I wanted to prove to myself that it was within my power to change.

---

[9] The lady who falls down in the commercial looks less old every day.

THE AMAZING BODY

My trainer marveled once at how resilient our bodies are. It almost seems like many people might as well be *trying* to break their bodies, shoving terrible things into them and doing nothing to keep them healthy. But the bodies keep hanging on—for a while.

Like many sixties' kids, I fell into the World Book Encyclopedia Volume "H" (nervous system, skeletal system, muscles, organs). Over and over, I'd flip those pages back and forth. It was fascinating. I actually snagged an "H" off eBay and still look at it.

I got to see a real body in a college anatomy class. It was very old: a woman in her seventies who had been preserved for twenty years, old enough that everything was the same shade of sallow mustard. But it was still exciting to see *real* organs and muscles. Looking at the cadaver, I had a pointy-high-heels Jesus moment; having spent her years in them, fashionable at the time, the bones in the woman's feet were deformed into a tight "V." They'd literally become wedged together. Volunteers were needed to lower the woman back into the embalming fluid, and as we did, someone let go unevenly, and her leg splashed into the fluid, which splashed onto my face. Good times.

I'd seen how the oldest bodies looked—and the youngest: I'd only viewed myself as a baby in pictures, but after the PBS series *The Body*, I instead saw the fascinating skeletal and spinal cord and electrical connections we're made of. Viewing my little body that way, knowing it carried within itself everything it would need to grow into a full-size human, struck me with awe. And the thought of all the terrible things I'd forced into it made me sad (e.g., drinking so much one night in northern Wisconsin and so damaging my nervous system that I was literally shaking during the long drive home). My adult body at thirty was no different from the precious one at three months, and I was trying to destroy it.

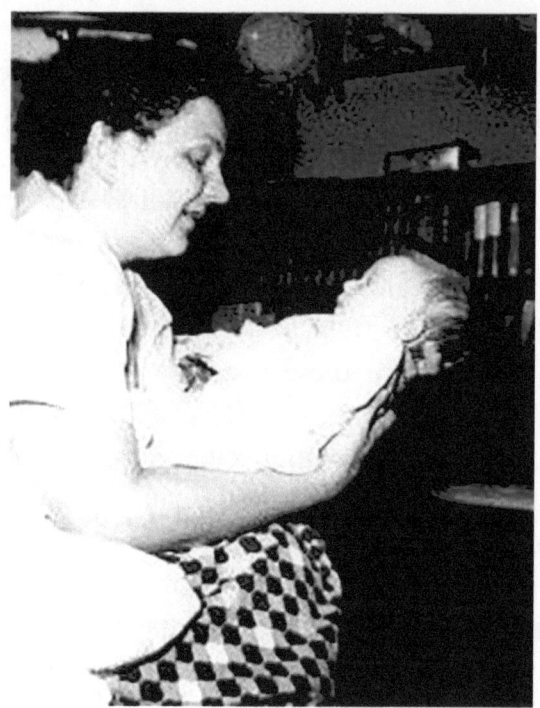
Our miraculous bodies

MY ORIGINAL BODY

I'd never felt truly comfortable in my body and often wondered what it was supposed to look like without all the extra fat dumped on it. (One of my affirmations included "I have no extra fat on my body.")

The concept of weight first reached its cruel arms out to me in sixth grade. It was "Weigh Day," and we all had to trudge down, boys and girls together, in alphabetical order (so I always had to go first) to the health room. With everyone watching, a nurse called out your weight for another to record. I wasn't terribly overweight as a kid, but it was an embarrassing exercise, and self-consciousness was spawned.

Like many girls, I found increasing fault with my body as I got older. Never mind having a nice smile, nice eyes, nice hair . . . all

I saw were a big bottom and big legs. By the time I got to junior high, I was so self-conscious that I dreaded walking down the hall in front of any boy I liked.[10] If I knew a boy was behind me (unavoidable bad pun) I'd quickly maneuver away or blend into the crowd. If there was no crowd, I was out of luck and just walked as fast as I could—which likely drew even more attention.

My body didn't look like I wanted it to, but sometime in high school, I had a weirdly clear vision of what my "good" body would be: walking into a bar like in old Westerns, wearing sleek black jeans that hugged my lean muscles. I probably saw something on TV or on the street, but that vision is still vivid sixty years later. And through the years, that singular vision remained my signpost as I went through periods when I weighed less and thought, *This is it—I'm finally realizing my vision!* But even during those times (maybe my stomach was reasonably flat), I realized I wasn't really there. Only after I started getting truly fit and saw the muscles in my body changing did I finally see how I was "made" to be. I was bringing vision into reality. It felt as good in real life as in that prescient vision.

If I'd had an unjustifiably bad image of my body for the first part of my life, my actions justified it for the second.

I was blessed with a pretty flat stomach (one of my high school friends was eternally jealous) but spent most of my adult life in belts and tight stonewashed eighties' jeans up to my waist, straining to contain my bloated stomach. Sometimes I was so full and bloated that I felt sick and looked pregnant. Friends and I were going to a Christmas party once when, an hour before, I caught myself sideways in the mirror, saw how pregnant I looked, and called to cancel. Instead of going out and having fun, I sat home with my big gut, feeling sick. I was so disgusted, I took a sideways picture but finally couldn't stand to look at it anymore and tore it up.

---

[10] I liked them all.

At my social services job in the 2000s, I was wearing size-fourteen jeans on a five-foot, three-inch frame. For lunch, I'd walk over to the one store in the depressed neighborhood food desert to get a bottle of chocolate milk and a can of ravioli. Or I'd run to the fast-food place on the corner for a taco "salad" that sounded healthy but wasn't much of a salad and came with a side of chili—all around 900 calories. These lunches were often accompanied by string cheese—it was "low-fat" after all! My body was getting bigger.

In April 2014, I wanted to get away and headed to Daytona Beach. My romantic vision of lounging on the beach was shattered as soon as I walked into the hotel room and caught myself in the mirror. Work stress had had me spending my days gulping Goldfish crackers, dry roasted peanuts, double-scoop ice-cream cones, greasy pizza *with* warm buttery seasoned biscuits, Subway sandwiches with potato chips, and Culvers.

I was moving farther and farther away from my original body.

CHAPTER 15

Weight

Weight is not a fitness goal or necessarily correlated to fitness. If you're eating and exercising well, whatever weight you are is appropriate. The goal is to be healthy. To have a strong heart and strong muscles and bones. To have veins and capillaries and lymph that run clean. To have cells fortified with nutrients instead of harmful substances.

But weight (too much or not enough) can be an indicator of overall health, and weight fluctuations can be an indicator of inconsistent health practices. My wild swings from bad eating and inadequate exercise tell the story, and the dips were as harmful as the rises.

FIRST UNHEALTHY WEIGHT DIP

In 1985 I decided I was going to get down to 118 pounds. I don't know why I picked that number, but I know why I wanted to do it. A friend's neighbor was giving away two pairs of size-eight pants in the signature deep pastel-pink and deep pastel-blue eighties' colors. It's a blur, and all I recall is not eating and smoking lots of pot. (Beer calories, of course, didn't count.) I did allow myself a piece of gum that tasted like Thanksgiving dinner. By God, I got into those pants—although I didn't stay in them long.

I was thin but far from healthy. Remembering Nan Gilbert's *The Unchosen*[11] helped me understand the difference. Ellen, the sweet but self-described "lumpy" main character, was raised in a caloric German beef stroganoff and apple strudel family. Her pen-pal boyfriend was planning a Christmas visit, and Ellen embarked on a reckless diet. The day before the expected visit, she bought a new dress, but she ended up weak and ill. Naturally, the guy didn't show, and she threw the dress into her closet. Fast-forward several months, and after starting a sensible eating plan, the specter of a real date arose. She returned to the dress, it fit like heaven, and she looked like an angel in it. A seed had been planted within me, and even in my most uncomfortable days, I never forgot her description of how putting that dress on again felt—this time on a *healthy* body.

SECOND UNHEALTHY WEIGHT DIP

My second weight dip was in the early nineties when I went to Boston with a friend. I was thin and looked great. But looks are deceiving. I hadn't traveled much, and maybe it was the excitement of a trip, but my stomach was so knotted that every couple of miles (literally) of walking, I had to find a bathroom to dry heave in. Sometimes just a few blocks. I do not know how my friend put up with it. For years, I was afraid to travel, thinking I'd go through the same thing. But subsequent trips proved I just hadn't been taking care of myself.

THIRD UNHEALTHY WEIGHT DIP

In the nineties, I was working as the office manager at a personal injury law firm in Boston. It was how one might imagine a small-injury law firm would be, and the stress was high. And after surviving thirteen years in a high-powered law firm where lawyers sat in running cars, with five minutes to get to the

---

[11] Nan Gilbert, *The Unchosen* (Ishi 2015).

airport (you could do that then), and you were thirty-nine floors up, finishing a one-hundred-page document for them on an old-fashioned five-by-seven floppy disk that could go "bad" at any moment, that's saying something.

At the personal injury law firm, I got stoned every morning, stopped next door at the Dunkin' Donuts for a blueberry crawler, drank coffee all day, went to lunch at Burger King for a Whopper with onion rings, went home to smoke more pot, and ate everything and anything I could find there—including a couple of Quaker Oats strawberry instant oatmeal packets for munchies. And the stress got so bad that I eventually couldn't eat at all, could only drink milk, and started wasting away. A coworker was worried and took me to a deli where he could only get a small carrot and spoonful of mashed potatoes down my throat.

Wasting away, with milk on my desk

FOURTH UNHEALTHY WEIGHT DIP

In 1999 I was working as the office manager/executive assistant at a large social services agency. It was two full-time jobs, I was insanely busy, and I lost twelve pounds in less than a year (before I put thirty-two back on the next year). I'd used a scale as a teenager but not as an adult. An early coworker had casually mentioned that she knew she needed to lose weight because her skirts were getting tight. Her comment stayed with me, and I'd adopted her method. Unfortunately, it didn't work. I could tell my clothes were getting looser but not tighter. The mighty power of denial.

CHAPTER 16

Mind Work

I had several solid reasons to fight back, but changes to my mindset happened gradually. They started as simple things but became increasingly profound:

Fat is gross. I watched the "skinny Oprah" show when she carted out globs of something on a platter representing fat. The image of those globs stayed with me and was further cemented when I read that one pound of fat equals five pounds of pressure on knees.

Irritation. Feeling bloated irritated me, and I didn't want to go through life irritated.

I wanted to create. I've always wanted to create something special—writing or painting or composing music—but the magic never came. Then I realized that if I couldn't create a piece of art, my body could be my canvas. My *body* was the work of art I could create and make beautiful.

I wanted my own work. There's a settler house in Random Lake, WI, called the Nowack Home. I love seeing the inside of the house and the garden, thinking about the basic tasks that comprised living in those days. I felt a pull to live that basically again. Not possible in today's world, but I came to see my health work as my "farm work"—my twenty-first-century tasks—as genuine and important as any were to the Nowacks.

I also wanted practical work. In November 2016 I thought about getting a nutritionist license until I saw the price tag. Instead, I found a twenty-pound tome at Half Price Books called *Understanding Nutrition.* I opened up a new notebook (my favorite thing to do) and dove in like my life depended on it: hunched over the desk, taking notes like I'd done in high school biology, memorizing terms, learning to calculate calories. My zeal lasted for three chapters. But taking back my health would be my practical work.

I wanted to feel young again. I'd never forgotten how it felt to be nine, running around the neighborhood for hours, going in only because it was too dark to see. The burning ball of nine-year-old energy in my chest had been trampled on but hadn't gone away. I wanted to feel that way again. I knew being sixty could never be like nine. But the glowing ball of energy was still inside me, and I wanted whatever remnants of it that were still there.

I felt an obligation to take care of my body. I think about the many people who haven't been graced with the fully functioning body I have. I'd seen them sitting with a loved one in the neurology department waiting room where I was undergoing Meige treatments,[12] some with bodies that twitched uncontrollably, some with no movement at all. Once, while driving home debating yet again whether I would or wouldn't work out, I saw a father helping his young son in leg braces navigate the sidewalk. I imagined what the thought of taking a relaxing run or spending half an hour in a gym would mean to them. I'm not crazy about the word "sin," but I believe that to not appreciate and care for my body would be a disgrace.

I wanted to be a winner. I wanted to be strong and prove I could meet life's challenges. I knew that taking care of my physical health was part of that. Starting on the fitness path made me begin to think differently about myself. I was captivated by a photo of a trainer with pure joy on her face and put it on my refrigerator with a card above that said, "I want to be a winner" in thick black letters. I *did* want to be a winner, whatever that meant. I'd hem and haw about whether I should do something. Then I'd see the photo and card, and it was no longer a matter of deciding. I wanted to be like the woman in the photo.

I wanted to take care of myself. I realized that fitness represented self-care, and self-care represented self-love. And even if self-care and self-love weren't my life's purpose, they put me in the right lane and positioned me for the ultimate goal: personal power.

I wanted to have personal power and realized that feeling lousy equaled a loss of power. I started to understand, when tempted to eat something bad for me, that it would mean giving up my power.

I wanted self-esteem. In a journal entry, I wrote that I felt "fat and not regarded." Not until many years later did I realize that the "regard" I wrote about was self-regard: the gift of self-pride, self-respect, self-esteem.

---

[12] A facial muscle disorder.

I wanted to be in control of my health and my body. When there's so much out of my control, it feels good to control what I can. When I was heavy and bloated, I felt irritated at myself for being out of control. I couldn't do anything about my face seemingly melting more each day as I aged, but I could control my health and body. And if I could take control of my health and body, I could take control of other things. Controlling my physical health was a metaphor for living a self-directed life.

I wanted to live a self-directed life. In April 2013, I read that phrase somewhere, and it stuck. That thought might not impress those already doing it, but for fifty-five years (and various reasons), I'd let myself be blown about by the winds of the world. I'd never planned what I would be or how I would be or even who I would be.

To illustrate just how aimless my life was, after several months of working my first post-high school job, I decided to move north of Milwaukee. Everything was in place, and a couple days before, a group of friends and I went to a bar to celebrate the start of my new life. A cute guy I'd liked in high school (remember I liked them all) was there and showed some interest in me. Obviously *because* I was moving! But I actually said, "Well, maybe I should stay here." So when I say blown about by the winds, I mean blown about by the winds.

The concept of living a self-directed life, probably a given for most people, was new for me, and I wanted it. Reading that one simple phrase made me see how I wanted to live. And part of living that way was directing my body and my health.

I wanted to move past anxiety. I spent the first fifty-five years of my life in a state of self-imposed anxiety. There were different reasons, but they manifested psychologically and physically. In the mid-eighties, a friend treated us to massages. She went first, and as I sat in the waiting room, I didn't hear a sound. When my turn came, I talked through the whole thing.

Not sure if I was just nervous because it was my first massage, but I certainly hadn't had the same relaxing experience my friend had. I didn't know how to be still and calm during it because I had no stillness and calm inside. The massage therapist also pointed out, not unkindly, that I walked with my chin stuck out: anxious, defiant, ready to battle the world. I absorbed what she said, and I began drawing my chin in and standing up straight. Getting fit would tackle pent-up anxiety.

I wanted to capture the present. In the early 2000s, I found a book that impressed me so much, I spent an hour at an office store copying it. I don't know the title, but it inspired me like Cat Stevens's "Sitting"—bringing into awareness our movement through life, in and out and around, finally back to the innermost part. The book contained existential messages of self-discovery that captured me—even though they'd take years to fully bloom within me.

Around 2018 or so, I began to finally understand what being present meant. I'd catch myself rushing through mundane tasks and suddenly stop short, wondering why I was rushing and where I was rushing to. I realized I was here, right now, and could imagine how much, when eighty-five, I'd yearn to have just one minute of here, right now, back—even if it was spent putting clothes in the washing machine or wiping down the kitchen counter. To have one precious minute again, looking out the kitchen window at the birds or snow gently falling. The enormity of this indescribable thing called life, *being alive*, would almost overwhelm me. Taking care of the healthy body accompanying me on my life journey became aligned with the very enormity of being part of life itself.

I wanted to die without regret. I thought about what regrets I might have in my final moments and knew that not taking care of myself would be the biggest. I knew there would be other inevitable regrets, but I didn't want living unhealthily to be one of them—especially when I had so much control over it. If I died, I didn't want it to be because of something I did or didn't do. I would feel like a fool if I ignored a second chance at a happy life.

I wanted to live with peace. "The world" for me means striving to be the best I can be. This includes taking care of my health and feeling strong and lean—the subconscious desire likely prompting the black jeans vision that had stayed with me through the years. To have peace, I needed to walk through the world's door before I left it. Taking care of my body and being my "best self" would take me through that door and bring me peace.

POINT OF DEPARTURE

The war with excess to recapture my health had begun, and my mind was ready. How to start? In 2015, I read Sarah Breathnach's Simple Abundance[13] in which she wrote about a point of departure—or as philosopher William James described it, starting with "as strong and decided an initiative as possible."[14] I'd been coming close to my point of departure by a June 12, 2014, journal entry: "I want to secure my physical future. It's like anything else—a decision. Do I really want it? Do I want to be elevated to the level 'above' common life—the level of wind and time—being in a universal state?"

Deciding to change was the crucial step, but I needed a solid, tangible demarcation line to step over into the brave new world.

---

[13] Sarah Ban Breathnach, *Something More* (Warner Books 1998), 37.
[14] Habit 1877

CHAPTER 17

Tactics

I'd reached my point of departure and was ready to change. How? Like I always had, I pulled out my metaphorical pencil and ruler, gathered my thoughts, and mapped out some tactics.

TACTIC 1: APPROACHING HEALTH AS A PROJECT

I decided to think about taking back my health as I would any work project and set clear, attainable goals. To keep from being overwhelmed at the start, I decided to do one healthy thing every day: drink two glasses of water, go one day passing up candy or pastries, stick with one helping of pasta. I put an inexpensive calendar on my kitchen table and recorded at least one daily "victory." Recording something positive that I did or something negative I avoided ensured I'd receive at least one star every day. I didn't buy stars but did draw them.

I started by focusing on food. Accepting that it would make me uncomfortable, I confronted the reasons and emotions behind my eating so much and recorded what I was going to do about each:

Work anxiety	Think of ways to streamline/adjust work tasks; have healthy snacking options on hand

Habit	Notice when I'm eating without being hungry and stop immediately; check if there are any emotions present when reaching for food—confront them without fear; make a list of other small, short-term things to do; do something physical
Trying to recapture childhood comforts	Be grateful for having good memories and move on and make new ones
Overcommitment	Set boundaries and decide which things I need to let go of
Treating myself	Realize that I'm hurting myself rather than helping myself; the real "treat to myself" is choosing health and being rewarded by the other things (control, self-esteem, etc.) that come with it

TACTIC 2: THINKING LIKE A CEO

Around 2014, I read *How to Become a CEO* by Jeffrey J. Fox.[15] I wanted to be the CEO of my health. Fox said to "regularly practice a solitary task to increase mental toughness," and he gave some examples of "hard and lonely tasks":

a) Studying late for a graduate degree

b) Running long distances in the early a.m.

c) Splitting wood

I'd done the first by finishing my masters—literally staying up the night before it was due by FedEx, drinking three pots of coffee. (not proud) And I was never going to split wood with my broken shoulders. But, like Goldilocks, the middle one was just right. His book had stayed with me, and I eventually adopted his *do something hard alone* suggestion through morning workouts.[16]

---

[15] Jeffrey Fox, *How to Become CEO: The Rules for Rising to the Top of Any Organization* (Hachette Books 1998).

[16] Another benefit of a hard workout in the morning is that it keeps me from getting wrapped up in stressful situations during the day. Thinking about the workout and the satisfaction I got from doing it can lift me out of a current situation and take me to a satisfying place.

Like Fox knew it would, workouts were giving me power and personal control that I could translate into other things, like fighting temptation. In the early days when I was so tempted at work to have junk food, I thought I'd lose my mind. I learned to fight against it with the same intensity I put into my workouts: I *will* finish this run. I *will* do the extra five reps. I *will* go out today even if I don't feel like it. And I *can* pass up this Krispy Kreme donut. The really interesting part is that when I'd get home, having resisted the temptation, I'd realize it hadn't really been that hard to pass up. It hadn't been a knock-down-drag-out fight. I'd simply been dealing with a "strong whim." If I wasn't able to stand up to a strong whim, where was I? Fox was right: Doing something hard alone makes other hard things easier. I did that. *I can do this.*

TACTIC 3: ENJOYING DEFERRED GRATIFICATION
Another way to build strength is to delay gratification. I don't know how other people learn this, but it wouldn't be a surprise that it hadn't been in my toolbox. I decided to try it. Instead of ripping open the bag of shredded cheddar cheese on the way home from the store, I waited. I came to realize that "looking forward to" getting home and dumping the heavenly shreds of fake-orange-colored cheese into my mouth was more satisfying—and even kind of fun. Then I understood that delayed gratification was so satisfying because it was about control—and control is power. Control and power took me to a place where I could not only decrease eating bad food but leave it behind completely. All simply by waiting.

TACTIC 4: EXPLORING THE SUBCONSCIOUS
I knew about the subconscious but wanted to go deeper and discovered Joseph Murphy's *The Power of Your Subconscious*

Mind.[17] Murphy's book was a clear, practical, straightforward guide to accessing it. His style and direct approach moved me from thinking of affirmations as New Age speak to a mechanical process: if you *do* this, this *will* happen. Affirmations are tricky, and I initially got caught in the "Is this really true? Do I really believe this? Am I just saying it? Am I fooling myself?" thing. But the only thing needed for affirmations to work is to *want* them to, and I started doing them daily. They changed and evolved depending on what was important to me, but they always included health:

- I have perfect health.
- I take care of the precious, miraculous body I have been given.
- I treat my body with love and care.
- I control my body.

My day does not start until I have said these affirmations and they have become part of my mind and my behavior. Even if some might argue that affirmations don't alter the subconscious, they do serve as practical, concrete grounding points.

TACTIC 5: BUILDING MOMENTUM

Getting healthy is like anything else. I had to do just enough to get in front of it or on top of it to keep going. I needed to be able to see the Promised Land. Even the smallest success kept me heading toward the next one. I knew I had to *just do something*. The biggest secret (the magic) to feeling amazing is that it's not magic. It's just a steady accumulation of small, good decisions. Often, after a long day at work, I'd pass up the "treat" of going for pizza or stopping for a grilled cheese and a beer. The next morning I'd reflect on how much better off I was without all that crap in my body and how easy it actually had been to pass it up. One small decision today, another tomorrow, and it keeps building. Unfortunately, it works the other way

---

[17] Joseph Murphy, *The Power of Your Subconscious Mind* (Bantam Books 2000).

too: one bad thing today, one bad thing tomorrow, and after a few days, you're feeling lousy again. It doesn't take long either way. But the point is the same: small decisions add up and build momentum no matter which way you're going.

TACTIC 6: LOOKING FOR GOOD EXAMPLES

One woman making a very good decision about her health could be spotted outside my window. She had this unusual gait between running and walking, her feet barely leaving the ground, slogging along, slow and steady. She was large, tall, and solid. I watched her for months, fascinated. And one day I noticed something: She was going a little faster, and there were almost imperceptible changes in her body. It was a special thing to watch. I loved how she kept at it—slogging along day after day, month after month, on the hottest days and on the coldest. I wondered what motivation was giving her such steely determination.

In the early eighties, I worked in a graphic arts place, and a designer gave me one of his drawings. I don't remember his name but wish I could give him a formal shout-out. I thought of this picture often when watching the running woman and in the early days of my fitness journey when I didn't feel like doing anything. The picture helped me visualize progressive, gradual change, and it made me understand that getting out and doing something, anything, would keep me going forward. I've moved to a different part of the city but still think about the running woman and hope she's well.

TACTIC 7: THINKING ABOUT FOOD IN A NEW WAY

Eating should be about taking in food and nutrients you enjoy, not blind habit. An unhealthy couple I knew planned trips according to the fast-food places they'd pass along the way: Denny's for breakfast, McDonald's for lunch, chips and cookies in the car for an afternoon snack, Arby's for dinner, snacks for the hotel. That's habit.

For decades, I heard (and ignored), "You are what you eat." But I found myself thinking about those majestic golden maples on the seminary grounds that had made me understand my place in the cycle of nature. And about plants. How many times have I seen what happens to a drooping plant when I water it? Five or ten minutes later, as if by magic, it's springy and standing tall. I wondered why my body would work any differently. And if water works that way, why not food?

In 2016 I discovered Amelia Freer's *Eat. Nourish. Glow.*[18] It was the *glow* that got me (like her publisher knew it would!). Freer is an English nutritionist, and her book caused a profound change in how I thought about food. Not only did my fifty-eight-year-old skin not glow—it looked seventy-five. (I might be exaggerating a little.) I had enough sense to know that the multitude of beauty regimens being hawked were worthless unless they were accompanied by nutritious food.[19]

I started to really think about what I was putting in my body, and it started with sugar. No matter how much money you spend on skin creams, you can't undo the cellular damage that sugar causes from the inside. Carbohydrates are converted to sugar that gets stored around organs.

I've heard that sugar is more addictive than some hard

---

[18] Amelia Freer, *Eat. Nourish. Glow.* (Thorsons 2015).
[19] I admit to ordering a fancy television skincare product. Of course I might as well have set my money on fire (although for those doing nothing, any kind of regimen is an improvement). I used to feel embarrassed about getting snagged, but now I view it with more affection. It represented my first attempts to take care of myself.

drugs. I smoked pot and did some other stuff that wasn't too addictive, so I can't say, but once I started significantly reducing the amount of sugar I ate, I could see its power.

I went just over a year without eating candy. It was easier than I thought. But I wasn't going to pass up chocolate a friend brought back from France. I'm not even going to pretend I tried to savor it (in my predelayed gratification tactic days). I gobbled it down. It was decadent and delicious. And the next day, I wanted more—I "needed" more. I grabbed a Reese's at the store that night. I got a hold of myself, but the intensity of the craving was wild.

Two or three times a year, I'd stop at Starbucks for a chai tea. After one of these stops, on the way to work the next day, I had an almost overwhelming urge to get another one. All it took was one damn cup of the stuff to so physically and psychologically affect me. So I can imagine how hard it must be for people who consume boxes of junk food to give them up. And I don't find it hard to believe that sugar is as addicting as some drugs. I knew I'd conquered it when I arrived home one night craving an orange. Nature's sugar.

In 2017 I got Freer's *Nourish & Glow: The 10-Day Plan*.[20] Because of her first book, I felt confident the second wouldn't be just another plan that sounds great but includes weird ingredients and is impossible to adopt. I was right. In "project mode," I sat down with the book and a notebook and fell in. The recipes were interesting but not exotic or hard (although you do need to know that aubergine means eggplant). Freer's book was the first time I thought about seriously changing my eating using a "plan." I stayed with it for several months, by which time I was on a more solid road to proceed with my own choices. Freer made me start thinking about food with reverence. Thank you, Amelia.

---

[20] Amelia Freer, *Nourish & Glow: The 10-Day Plan* (Michael Joseph an imprint of Penguin Books 2017).

TACTIC 8: JUST STOPPING

My dad set an example I never forgot. Although he didn't really overindulge in anything, he did like Diet Pepsi. One day he stopped buying it, and when I asked why, he said he was drinking too much of it. When I asked why he didn't just drink less, he said he was either going to have it or not have it. That seemed like a radical approach, but all these years later, I understand. It's too easy to form a habit and too hard to break one. I internalized this principle and have simply made decisions to stop things that are bad for me. Excess of any kind is physical abuse. I wouldn't let anyone else physically abuse me, so why would I physically abuse myself? For that matter, why would I make anything harder on myself than I have to? Just stop.

TACTIC 9: THROWING STUFF AWAY

If I couldn't just stop, I had a crazy backup tactic: If I felt that I just absolutely had to have something, I'd get it, have some, and throw the rest away.

I started doing this in Boston, addicted to cigarettes but desperately not wanting to be. The "buy a pack in the morning and a pack in the evening and throw them away after two smokes" routine. As ridiculous as it sounds, it kept me from falling all the way back in.

Same for food. If I really, really wanted something that was bad for me, I'd eat half and throw the rest away (sometimes going as far as making sure it was mixed in enough with garbage to keep me from grabbing it back out!). Several Sendik's cherry pie halves met this grisly fate. Changing habits is about doing whatever you have to do until you don't have to anymore.

TACTIC 10: SETTING FIFTEEN-MINUTE GOALS

Professor Virginia Valian described in her "Working It

Out"[21] piece that she suffered a debilitating work block while completing her PhD. To tackle it, she began working in daily fifteen-minute increments, knowing she could last at least that long. I've used her tactic often—not all instances being exactly fifteen minutes but with a solid start and stop.

The first time was giving up candy and cheese for Lent in 2018. Forty days instead of fifteen minutes, but a definitive length of time and end I knew I could stay with. And just long enough to break the habit. (Guess it takes fifty-nine to seventy days to form one.)

My next fifteen-minute goal was "slimming down" for a dream trip to Germany and Austria in December 2019—a three-month goal that started in October.

Next was the COVID goal. Three months after returning from Germany, COVID hit. Never shying away from a reason to indulge in excess, I used it as an excuse to be "bad" and blew up from 119 to 134 pounds in five months. The watershed moment came at my annual physical when my doctor suggested a statin for my skyrocketing cholesterol.

Last stop before the world ended. Reese's, of course.

---

[21] Virginia Valian, "Learning to Work," in *Working It Out 23 Writers, Artists, Scientists, and Scholars Talk About Their Lives and Work*, ed. Sara Ruddick and Pamela Daniels (Pantheon 1977), 163-178.

The thought of the rest of my life filled with pills was the second time I had the *fuck* scared out of me. I set the largest fifteen-minute goal yet by asking the doctor to give me six months to see what I could do by myself and turned to a strict Mediterranean diet.[22] Six months later, I'd lost fourteen pounds and reduced my cholesterol by forty-seven points. The doctor was astonished, and I was relieved. All I was doing was going forward to a solid goal, eating great, and moving my body. And none of it had been that hard.[23]

The fifteen-minute goals established focus and made me feel good when I reached them. But the tactic has even greater power: I can do anything in "bites"—no matter how long the bites are. I sent Professor Valian an email of thanks, and she kindly replied that she was happy the piece she'd written almost fifty years before was still helping.

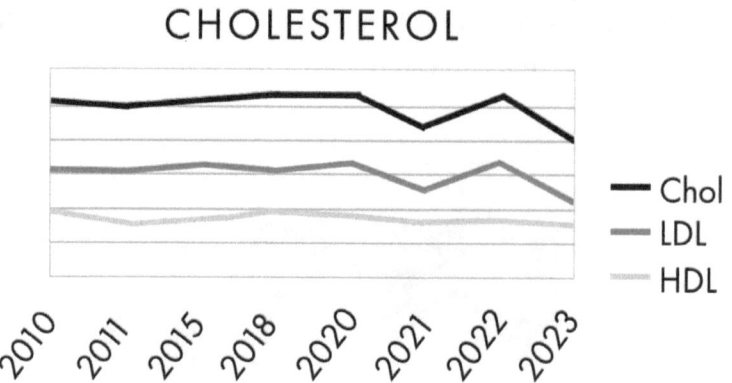

---

[22] America's Test Kitchen, *The Complete Mediterranean Cookbook* (America's Test Kitchen 2016)—the most comprehensive and beautiful book I've seen.

[23] Another 2022 increase before I got on the good cholesterol train forever. I was only in stage four of my five stages of change—not quite to the Promised Land yet.

TACTIC 11: SETTING SOLID LONG-TERM GOALS

Some goals need to be longer—in fact, open-ended. In January 2021, I identified the three I wanted for my life: to be secure, vital, and fit. Secure in my job, financially, and in my home. Vital, participating in and contributing to the world. Fit, being physically healthy and enjoying my body.

I wrote that simple yet profound trio on a piece of paper and posted it on the wall next to my desk with a statement: "Treat every moment with care." I had my sights set and was ready for the longest fifteen-minute health goal of all: forever.

PART IV

RECOVERY

CHAPTER 18

Physical Work

Having the motivation, changing my mindset, and developing tactics were crucial, but the physical work was next. I can still feel the shock when I saw my trainer's first workout for me: walk briskly for twenty minutes. I'd made the decision to start training, I'd paid the money, and I was excited. But I had to actually *do something*!

Trying to recount how I took back my health in a strict chronology would be messy—probably impossible. I did some things for a while, stopped, started again, and added some other things. But sharing my journey by topic describes the path well enough.

BREATHING

How often I'd heard "the breath of life," but the phrase became real for me when someone I knew died from diaphragm cancer. The diaphragm is a fascinating part of the body: an umbrella-shaped muscle under our lungs that contracts when we inhale to pull the air into them. I think about people in the 1950s with polio who spent months, some even years, lying on their backs in iron lungs, staring at the ceiling. I often think of them when I breathe.

In the late 2000s, after my third shoulder surgery, I thought massages would help my shoulder muscles, and the masseuse observed that I wasn't really breathing—not deeply. It was the first time anyone had pointed it out, and I was still years away from understanding its real significance, but, like so many other things, it planted a seed. Good health depends on good breathing. I eventually came to understand the beauty of making my diaphragm and lungs healthy and strong and always make a point to breathe deeply.

WATER

Once I know what I want or have to do, I approach it with steel discipline. *Except drinking more water.* The fact that water comprises 60 percent of our bodies and streamlines all our functions, from blood cells to brain usage, continually impressed me, and I'd been trying for years to drink more of it. I probably recorded more than 100 times in my journals "*DRINK MORE WATER!*" I lugged jugs to work, used them for a couple days, then stopped. I tried keeping a cup next to my kitchen faucet. At work, I vowed to alternate one cup of coffee with one cup of water. I'd think about the drooping plants that spring up when watered. I noticed Justin Bieber had a huge water bottle during his carpool karaoke with James Corden. I saw a quote from Lady Gaga's manager about how she drinks water throughout the day to avoid looking worn (good God, if she can look worn, what must I look like?). But I still didn't drink enough water. When you're thirsty, it's like God's nectar. When you're not, *it's so hard to drink.*

Then it happened. I strained a muscle in my leg, and the inflammation took six months to subside. Feeling desperate, I finally exercised that discipline of steel and began drinking fifty-six ounces every day at work, even if it meant slamming down what was left before I let myself go home. I'll never know whether it was the water or coincidence that brought about my recovery. And there are current debates over just how much water we need every day. Coincidence or not, I will forever continue the practice of drinking *lots* of water because I could tell in only one day how much better I felt. Like a bright, springy plant in the sun.

STRETCHING

Muscles are so interesting. My brothers used to walk around the house flexing their biceps, but I never really understood what was happening until my college anatomy class. I was fascinated by seeing the different kinds of muscles through a microscope, but even that didn't solidify the connection between studying them and controlling my own. One of my friends in the eighties used to do a lot of stretching while we watched TV. She'd stretch while I sat on the couch stoned. Watching her made an impression on me, but I still didn't think of my body in a thoughtful, reverent way. My body was just something that carried me around.

It would take me thirty more years to make the link between muscles as an academic exercise and understanding how stretching them every day keeps them healthy and strong. But even back in 1986, I was inspired enough by muscles to make a homemade Christmas card about them:

The result of not taking care of my muscles hit when I moved in 2015. I was only moving a mile away and spent a day going back and forth, down the stairs and up the stairs. By early afternoon, my left leg started to tighten, and within a half hour, I couldn't bend it—the lactic acid had built up, and the muscles literally stopped working. Even though I had a whole week to move, I still wasn't smart enough to stop for the day. I kept pushing on (that nasty excess habit), continuing to make the trips with a straight leg. Even though I had the abstract interest in and appreciation of how muscles worked, tying that concept to taking care of my own wasn't there. The Prussian workhorse just kept working.

I now never end the day without getting on the floor and stretching. I never miss it. If I'm really tired, I still *do something*. And it should be no surprise that this simple practice has become one of the nicest parts of my day—stopping and reflecting and taking a few minutes to be good to myself and the marvelous tissues that hold me up and help me move.

YOGA

People who practice yoga "get it"—those who don't . . . run (for the hills). When people say yoga isn't for them, I think they weren't lucky enough to have the right teacher.

I don't know why, but I decided to give yoga a try in 2005, the challenge being how to do it with two shoulder surgeries behind me. I found Susan Apthorpe, a seventy-five-year-old Kripalu-trained instructor, who taught a class called Yoga Made Bearable. I was nervous and worried about feeling embarrassed. But Susan had a gentle approach and began each class by identifying people's physical issues so she could modify moves. I also had an honest-to-god yoga angel right next to me: an impossibly awkward man who struggled so hard it hurt to watch, but who kept coming every week for more torture. He carried me through.

Anyone who thinks yoga isn't a workout has never done it. As gently as I began, every muscle in my body screamed for two days. I understood by that time that the screaming was my body crying for help, a sign of my accumulated abuse. The yoga magic didn't happen right away, but eventually I fell into the rhythm and captured the joy. It only took doing it at a moderate level once or twice a week to feel the change in my body and muscles. No pulled this or that, no grunts or groans. And with relaxed muscles come the waves of spontaneous, satisfying big breaths that arrive out of nowhere. After doing it for a good while, I was able to practice on my own, but being part of a group in the early days was helpful.

But the real power of yoga is more than the physical changes. It's about stopping. Stop the world; I want to get off. Or at least take a break. I once told Susan that I felt too impatient to just stop, and she explained that that's exactly when I most needed to. Yoga is about doing only one thing in a moment. You end class by settling your body into the floor in Savasana: fully relaxed, with a clear mind. When you're done, you don't walk out the door—you float.

Locations do enhance classes. Mine began in a meeting room in a library but moved to the gym in the gorgeous St. Francis Seminary, an architectural treasure on the Milwaukee lakefront. I lived only a mile away and spent many warm sunny Sunday mornings walking there. Sometimes classes were on the grass overlooking the lake, with a deer or two joining. Combining nature with the care of body and mind is profound.

When my shoulder dislocated again in 2006, I had to give formal yoga up. But I've kept it close to my heart and found the best yoga DVD ever: *Gentle Yoga with Jane Adams*.[24] It's like taking an actual class—without crazy pretzel poses.

---

[24] Jane Adams, "Gentle Yoga" copyright 2011.

WALKING

Breathing deeply, drinking water, and stretching are good, but I knew I needed to start *moving*. As with everything I do, I went "all in" and, around 2013, checked out a hiking club. I signed up but never went because I realized I could walk in pretty spectacular places on my own, and I figured it was probably just a singles thing.

So, in 2014, like Forrest Gump, I started walking—and walking and walking. The first thing I did when I got home from work was change clothes and head out. Up and down the tree-lined streets of my neighborhood in a large triangle between my house, the lakefront, and the seminary grounds. I took walking "trips" around my extended neighborhood: sunscreen slathered on, hat, shorts with a pocket for keys, and a mini bottle of water. Some of those first walks might have been six or seven miles, and as I got closer to home, I felt like a little kid who wants to get picked up because they just can't take one more step.

Something very deep was driving my desire to walk. Sometimes even I was surprised at how I attacked it. Every summer, I head to northern Wisconsin for an overnight stay at the Silvercryst in Wautoma. It's a beautiful area and an excellent supper club, but I go for the long pier. In the middle of the night, I lie on it and stargaze.

One evening I was getting ready for my annual high-caloric dinner (and Southern Comfort Old-Fashioned) when something stopped me. Instead of eating, and as if out-of-body, I watched myself put on my tennis shoes (that I'd never before thought to bring on a trip) and, in a weird daze, headed out the door. It was an unpleasant evening—windy, unseasonably cold, overcast, drizzling. I walked, head into the wind, as if being pushed forward. I was Jane Eyre or *Wuthering Heights*' Kathryn, fighting the buffeting winds on the desolate English moors. *I was so determined to change the way I lived.* I walked for a couple miles and turned around. Later, on the pier, looking up at the now clear sky and sparkling stars, no heavy meal sitting in my stomach, with extra money in my wallet, I felt surprised and exhilarated. I saw something in myself that I hadn't even known was there.

Determined to walk

One of my routine walks took me past a lush copse of trees populated in spring by starlings. I loved walking by, having the birds dance around my head like Snow White skipping through the forest. Only later did I realize the birds were guarding their nests and dive-bombing me. The power of positive thinking!

I walked for years. Having transitioned to other things, it's endearing to look back at all the time and effort I put into it. I now enjoy running more than walking, although nothing will ever top a slow amble on a beautiful, warm, sunny October day, surrounded by glittering red, orange, and gold leaves, watching the squirrels scurrying around, hiding nuts for winter. But something had told me how good those walks were for me, and they set the stage for what would follow.

REAL AEROBICS

I'd done lots of eighties aerobics that I loved. I guess it was the line dancing thing—fun to move together in a coordinated group—and my old vague dream of being a dancer. But I never knew what real aerobics were until I started classes at Blast Fitness in 2018 with Jim (one name, like Jesus—or Cher!). From my machine workouts, I'd hear the near-deafening shouts from his class, and I regret not taking advantage of them sooner, especially because they were free with membership. I worked all day and just wanted to get my workout done.

Jim must have been in his late sixties but had the heart and energy that comes from feeling good and being happy. My trainer even knew him and said that people had been taking his classes for years. Jim's classes were the perfect combination of super moves and hard workout (no muscle left unburned) and ended with a mini yoga session cooldown, accompanied by his favorite music. Everyone left feeling completely spent but walking on air. He was even more inspiring because he wore a knee brace through it all.

Jim cared about every person in his class. When you joined, he asked when your birthday was and, at the beginning of each class, announced it. When my birthday came, I shared that it was my sixtieth (applause). I added with great sincerity that his classes had transformed my health (more applause). It was true.

One day as I checked in, I heard the front desk telling someone on the phone that "he didn't have any more information." In the aerobics room, everyone was standing solemnly around Jim. Blast was going out of business in two days, and this would be the last class. It felt like a wake for an unexpected death, and I wasn't even one of the people who'd been with him for so many years. At the end of the class, with great sadness in his voice, he said simply, "Okay, that's it, folks." I was disappointed but also panicked, not knowing how I was going to recapture the high intensity of those classes. It was little wonder that further on I'd fall in love with high-intensity training.

A secret I learned from doing aerobics? Doing something all-in is easier than doing something halfway. I realized this in one of those early eighties' sessions when, for some reason, I felt uninspired, my arms and legs too heavy to lift. Something made me gear up, and I could immediately feel how a little bit of energy produced more. This principle works for everything.

CHAPTER 19

Trainers

I had my fifth shoulder surgery in 2011 and spent years being scared to even lift something. I did not trust my shoulders. We don't think about how it feels to have our arms and legs connected to our body by ligaments and muscles, but I've spent a large part of my life knowing how it feels not to have the connection. It's like there's blank space in my shoulder, a lightness or emptiness where something should be. I have that same empty feeling in my right hip (no surprise, I'm sure those 2,000 backbends or splits screwed that up too). Everything I'm doing now will help me with other parts of my body someday.

Walking was good, but I knew I needed professional help to make my body and joints strong again—at least as strong as they could be. I've never spent lots of money on designer clothes or $6 coffees, and I viewed getting a trainer as a wise (and critical) monetary investment in my future. It was the most important decision I'd ever make.

MEDIOCRE TRAINERS

I tried professional training in the 2000s before my shoulder dislocated again in 2008. As a gym member, training was free or very low cost. Only now, having worked with a "real" trainer, can I see that the quality of the training matches the price. To be gracious, my first trainers were how someone described hair stylists in a chain: they're not bad; they're just new. I'd only had two surgeries and thought my shoulder problems were behind me. But that said, I knew how careful I had to be and tried my best to explain my situation. I might as well have been speaking in Klingon because I was put aboard the training train with cookie-cutter routines, rotating among all the machines, some of which I now know I probably shouldn't have been doing.

I did have a brief experience with a real trainer named Bill, a referral from my yoga teacher. I'd come to trust her, so I trusted her recommendation. Bill took me to a "real" gym (one I'd imagine Rocky at) and showed me safe routines. But he was still just a temporary consultation, not "my trainer."

A REAL TRAINER

Fate had smiled on me in 2009 when my first random call to find a physical therapist after my third surgery led me to Bill Lois, owner of Southern Lakes Physical Therapy (now Thera Dynamics Therapy in Bay View, WI). Bill and his staff guided me through physical therapy, and he understood how bad my shoulders were despite the "repairs": I couldn't lift a one-pound weight during my first visit. When I was ready for a trainer in 2014, I asked Bill for a recommendation, and he led me to John Andrews, owner of Bay View Fitness. Because they have such outstanding customer service, Bill reached out directly to John to explain my extraordinary situation.

The first meeting with John was a free consultation during which we talked about my physical history, lifestyle, activities, what I was putting into my body, and present and future fitness goals (mine were to get healthy and keep my shoulders in their sockets). You can always tell when people are truly listening to you, and he was. That sounds like a low bar, but it's the highest. He gave me two lists: healthy food and bad food. Short of seeing a nutritionist, I was thrilled to know my training would be comprehensive. The training series included a weekly gym session, varying individualized workouts for the week, and communication/advice as needed. I've included many examples of the knowledge John shared over the years, but it would be impossible to explain how much guidance, support, and confidence he's given me.

In 2014 I did a series of eleven one-hour sessions from April to June but stopped in 2015 and 2016, probably because of my job that included a daily two-hour commute. Back working in Milwaukee in 2017, I resumed and switched to eleven half-hour sessions. I was trying to keep the cost down, and thirty minutes is still a good workout. Training costs money, but I knew it was critical to getting strong again and avoiding another agonizing shoulder dislocation (the hardware is only as good as the supporting muscles around it).

I spent those first couple training years going through the motions faithfully enough, but I still hadn't crossed the total fitness line—I was working out but still eating badly.

By 2022, I was gaining good momentum and starting to feel better than I ever had even as a young adult. My trainer and I talked about setting goals, and to prepare for an October 10-k, I did three training series in a row.

The 2023 plan was a spring series to prime for summer-fall running and a fall

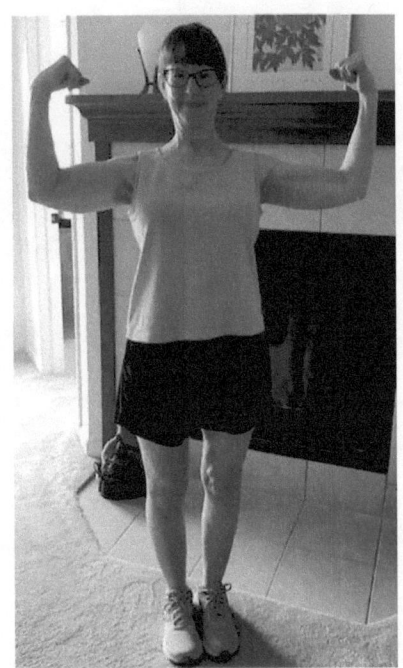

Sixty-fourth birthday – "on the way"

series to focus on machine and body work. Ramping down was John's suggestion and reinforces my belief that a true trainer looks out for a client's best health interests instead of trying to make money.

CHAPTER 20

Training Places

THE GYM

I'd had my Bally's membership since 1985 and used the gym for aerobics, machines, and swimming. But using a gym on your own and using a gym with a real trainer are very different experiences.

After I'd recovered from the shock in the early days of realizing I'd actually have to do something, my trainer introduced me to the elliptical. It was the gateway to really moving my body and was perfect for me. Looking back after having moved on to running and other workouts, the elliptical seems like a lot of effort for not much result. But in those early days, I was nervous about my shoulders, and the machine gave me confidence to begin using them again. I attacked that machine and even had some of the dopamine highs I'd heard about.[25] Now, when I see ellipticals in a gym window, I have a flood of warm memories, remembering the countless times I drove there after work on cold, snowy nights, determined to make my health and my life better. And thinking about how I felt walking out after, feet not really touching the ground, a strong and better me.

Walking into a gym with all the crazy-looking contraptions

---

[25] Best elliptical music: Brian Eno's *Taking Tiger Mountain (By Strategy)* (perfect warm-up, high intensity, cooldown order).

was intimidating. And despite having the gym, I hadn't used them much—only aerobics and a few simple machines until my shoulder came out again and everything screeched to a halt. If you move your muscles in a steady, controlled way, doing more in weight or reps, changes happen. The secret is to be present, slow, steady, and even. After working with a real trainer, I notice when people do workouts with fast, jerky movements, and I want to run over and show them how to do it. (I don't.) I plodded along on the machines and weights, day after day, month after month, and watched my muscles start to emerge.

I'd always gone to the gym after work, but when I became more serious about my health, I started going in the morning. Most of my working life was spent in places that started at 8 a.m., and it was great to finally work somewhere with a 9 a.m. start. I've always gotten up around 5:30 a.m. and have come to love the morning hours. Driving home from the gym one frigid snowy morning at 7:30 a.m., with Offenbach's *Barcarolle* from "The Tales of Hoffman" on the radio and winter sunlight streaming through the window, I thought, *This might be what heaven is like.*

Using the gym early also means that most of the machines are free, and there's something fun about being the only one there. My personal gym. Getting the workout out of the way also leaves me *free* for the rest of the day, instead of having to spend ten hours thinking about working out.

FIRST RUN

Like most kids, I ran around from morning to night. I can still feel myself bending over, hands on my knees to catch my breath for the next burst. It all stopped somewhere around seventh grade, and for the next forty years, I had dreams about trying to run but not being able to, like my shoes were cement. So, when I read my trainer's first running workout, I felt shocked:

DAY 1: five- to ten-minute warm-up + run for one min + walk for three mins. Repeat for twenty to thirty minutes. Walk backward for five minutes. Five-minute cooldown + stretching.

It's a pretty tame workout, but I would have to run! I planned to walk to South Shore Park as a warm-up and take off running on the first footfall into the park. The adrenaline was building in my body, and my heart was pumping faster and harder as I approached. I felt like I could hear it through my chest. I hadn't run in forty years, and I was about to. This was the moment. As I stepped onto the path, I took off full speed and couldn't believe how amazing it felt—for thirty seconds. After which I pretty much couldn't breathe. But I'd done it. I'd taken my first run. And a couple of months later, I realized that my dreams of not being able to lift my feet had stopped. The subconscious is a mysterious reservoir, and I believe mine was holding my joy of moving safe for me until I was ready to rediscover it.

BEING A "RUNNER"

I'm not proud to admit that I internalized the social snideness about "joggers" that was rampant in the late seventies: Joggers wore goofy little shorts and huge tennis shoes and headbands, and they seemed "obsessed" with health. (Rich, given how readily I'd embraced the ridiculous aerobics outfits of the eighties.) I hate that I was so swayed by public opinion, and I still don't know the reason for the public ridicule. My trainer suggested that criticism is the natural reaction of people who don't take care of their health. Friends can share that they did this amazing thing at work or finished an amazing project, but when you share something you did health-wise, it's considered vanity instead of an accomplishment. Pointing out sculpted arms is conceited—despite all the work that went into making them that way. Remembering my irrational feeling about joggers taught me to honestly explore judgmental reactions I have to something.

RUNNING INSIDE

My running got intense three months before the trip to Europe in December 2019. Twenty-five years of medical bills had kept me from doing much traveling, but I'd finally booked the "dream trip" to Germany and Austria. In my teens, I had a vivid image of going to Germany, probably a combination of vague heritage remnants, like my dad listening to polkas in the living room (while my mom watched ballets on PBS in the den), German classes in school, and the general lure of beer halls and gemütlichkeit prevalent in Milwaukee. The dream was finally going to happen, and I wanted to "look good." To prepare, for three months every day after work, often in the frigid, snowy darkness, I drove twenty minutes each way to run on the treadmill for thirty minutes while watching closed-captioned *Seinfeld* reruns.

I went from 130 to 119, and my knees held out during the trip—walking sixteen miles in three days from castle to castle. And I was still so energized that, the day after I got back, I went on a Sunday morning 6 a.m. run. But it caught up with me: my knees started to scream, and sometimes, even though they were fine on the treadmill, I could hardly step off. When I started another training session that spring, my trainer explained that doing the same thing over and over breaks knee joints down instead of making them stronger. He added that running on a slanted track also isn't good because of the repetition and angle; running outside is better because of the varying surfaces.

I still use the treadmill here and there in winter, popping a CD in my old-fashioned player, looking out the window without having to worry about uneven surfaces, watching the time and distance go up, feeling like I could go on forever, enjoying the satisfaction of reaching my goal, pushing the bright red STOP button, then the delicious cooldown. But I realized I needed to move into the world of outside running, where many joys awaited.

RUNNING OUTSIDE

There will always be a special place in my heart for my first running route. It was a nondescript street named Bolivar, a lackluster road dotted with small businesses and a trucking company on the north side, with a wide-open field on the south side hugging the north end of the Milwaukee airport. I guess I came to love that long, stark road because it symbolized my no-nonsense "this is business" determination to take my health back. I always got a little excited when I approached the corner where I transitioned from my walking warm-up into the run. I continue to love this preworkout heart-beating adrenaline rush, especially for high-intensity workouts where you know that *in just five seconds*, you're going to throw yourself into your highest possible physical limit.

Before I knew about pacing, I'd start off too fast and get winded, but I always fought to conquer that long barren stretch ahead of me. Because it was such an open area, I often had to fight strong winds. Getting to the end of those desolate blocks symbolized my bare-boned determination. I've also always liked planes, and having them practically skim my head as they came in was thrilling. In 2020 we had an unseasonably seventy-degree November day, and I was so sad to "lose" my road to the cold winter that I took a photo.

As September arrived with less light by the time I got home from work, I felt I needed to find a less remote route. They say that when a door closes, a new one opens, and I discovered the many joys of neighborhood running: seeing the creative ways people style their homes, people walking their dogs (sometimes the dogs walking them), a friendly "hey" to people passing, watching the progress of their flowers in the spring.

But I will always love my first road. I wonder what it will feel like to be eighty-five, going back to see that road, thinking about how good life was.

RUNNING FASTER

I moved into longer runs for my new fifteen-minute goal of finishing a 10-k (6.2 miles) in September 2022. After that was accomplished, my trainer incorporated faster runs into my workouts. I was leery because I always battled the usual joint pains that come with using my body. But go figure, running faster is actually easier on joints than running slowly.

Running fast is more satisfying in general, but especially going as fast as I can for *one minute*! Even writing that triggers my adrenaline. I needed a smooth place and was lucky to have a park with a large perimeter close by. A quarter-mile warm-up walk and a half-mile run brought me right to the entrance for takeoff. Running for one minute doesn't sound that challenging, but if you're doing it right, you panic around thirty seconds and feel like you'll die around forty-five. But then there's only fifteen to go! Fifteen seconds! And exhilaration when you reach sixty and transition to the slow run, walk, and float back home.

Last one in, but I did it!

    Running as fast as I can for one mile is also fun. Same warm-up, and then take off! And it's always the same. The exhilarating first quarter-mile, next quarter a little harder and wondering why I ever thought I wanted to do this, next quarter hanging on but vowing never to do it again, and then the final "oh my god, I'll never make this." But during the last quarter, I think, *It's only three blocks*! If I were being chased, I'd sure as hell want to be able to run three blocks pretty damn fast! And then the satisfying feeling of the watch buzzing on my wrist. And the heavenly wind down and satisfaction for my body, mind, and soul.

I knew I'd arrived when a friend and I were trying to catch a tour bus in DC. I was going to run ahead to hold the bus. It probably wasn't quite a mile but pretty close, and I was so in the zone that I ran right past the bus and only realized I'd gone too far when I was almost at the Capitol (our destination!). I turned back, and my friend and I arrived at the bus together. But it was proof that I was making a true difference to my health.

A WATCH

A nice thing about running is that it doesn't cost anything. As I progressed, though, I bought a good watch. I'd been going out a lot, sometimes faster, sometimes slower, and I wanted to have a better picture of what I was doing. The seed of self-competition had sprouted. I wanted to push myself, and the watch helped me do that.

I loved being able to see solid numbers. When I was newer, my goal might be to get to fifteen, and when I did, I felt like Rocky. Then getting down to thirteen, then twelve—always working down toward the ten-minute mile goal. And seeing the distance in tenths rise as I started going farther and farther was also rewarding and made me want to fight harder—*I can make it!* Having a watch is helpful, fun, and a good investment.

CLOTHES

I spent my early years running in the wrong clothes, thick cotton T-shirts that got more damp with every step I took and a sweatshirt (for "cold weather") that got so heavy and hot, I felt like a grizzly bear. Designer workout clothes aren't necessary—just a material that wicks moisture.

MOVING MEDITATION

Like yoga, meditation is about taking time in the day to jump off the crazy train and just be, just exist—without thoughts, opinions, worries, preconceived notions, nothing—returning to the core, whatever that means to someone. People experiment with mantras, but when I meditate, I sit completely in the moment, enjoying the energy flowing in my body.

When I run, I'm also completely present. The only thing I'm focusing on is putting one foot in front of the other. I also think about how strong my heart and bones and muscles are getting. Running is meditative and wonderful. Then I discovered something even better.

HIGH-INTENSITY WORKOUTS

Eventually, my trainer suggested we add high-intensity workouts. For the greatest benefit to my body and to save money, we'd do one series of high-intensity workouts in April to June, I'd keep working by myself through the rest of the year, and then we'd do a second strength building session in winter at the gym.

High-intensity workouts burn more calories in a short amount of time, metabolism stays high for hours after, oxygen consumption is improved, and heart rate and blood pressure are reduced. They might feel harder when you're doing them, but they're also more satisfying. The goal and best part of high-intensity workouts is reaching the point of pure exhaustion. Not just getting tired, not just thinking I won't be able to go on—but pure exhaustion, like a deflated balloon.

My first high-intensity workouts were on *the hill*—a steep rise along Lake Michigan—running up it as fast as I could and walking back down quickly. Then doing it four more times. Didn't sound too daunting, and the first time was okay. Second time was still good but harder. Third, slowed down a little, started to suffer, and wondered how I'd ever be able to do another one. Fourth, I hated my trainer. Fifth, *Goddamn it. I can do one more!* Then I was so tired, I almost felt sick. Then pure joy. It's all about the fight—and I'd won. And five times up the hill soon became ten.

But my next high-intensity workout is my favorite. Run one-half of a track lap as fast as I can, walk the other half back—then nine more times. It's stunning to see how much progress even a novice can make in a short amount of time—getting faster each week:

WEEK 1

1	2	3	4	5	6	7	8	9	10
7.4	9.05	8.55	9	9.1	7.5	8.45	8.5	7.1	9.1

WEEK 2

1	2	3	4	5	6	7	8	9	10
7.3	9.05	6.2	6.25	6.3	8.4	8.05	7.1	7.4	7.3

WEEK 3

1	2	3	4	5	6	7	8	9	10
5.5	6.15	6.1	6.1	7.15	6.45	7.5	6.35	9.25	7.25

High-intensity training makes me tough. And speaking of tough, I simply must share my colonoscopy prep story—yes, really! This is a big deal for me (Mom had it once, Dad twice). I've always felt grateful to have this as my health legacy because it's one I have a lot of control over with diet and testing. But oh, the dreaded testing. There are more expensive ways to prep with less drinking, but I've always opted to keep the extra $70 in my pocket and glug. But after years of enduring this agonizing ritual, this time was different.

As I stood at the kitchen counter, preparing for the first glass of misery, a thought appeared. *What if I treat this like a high-intensity workout?* I made eight marks on a piece of paper and, instead of drinking, slammed the liquid down and x-ed the first mark. I set the fifteen-minute timer and waited for the next "round." Slam, mark, set timer, wait. Slam, mark, set timer, wait. And instead of spending the fifteen minutes waiting and dreading the next round, I felt the old workout adrenaline rising and waited for my next chance to "kill it." It had never been so easy. High-intensity training had spilled over into colonoscopy prep—and every other thing in life that's difficult.

THE TRACK

I'd been doing all my workouts on city and neighborhood roads, but I wanted something smoother, and my trainer suggested a local high school track. I hadn't done track in school (too busy smoking and drinking), but the moment I walked onto that smooth black surface, I was home. I liked that the surface was softer on my older joints. I also liked having solid markers to focus on. But as important as these practical things are, they don't capture the full experience of using the oval. My first footfall onto that track, and I already felt like a winner.

I love going on Sunday afternoons when everyone else in the world is out doing something else. My trainer once mentioned the kind of weird satisfaction of working hard when others aren't. But I also like those surreal times when no one is out and I feel like I'm the only person on Earth, imagining myself viewed from above as just a small dot circling around and around the black oval.

The track is most majestic in the morning, when the sun has just cleared the horizon. When I'm done, I step off to meet the day—the sun now high and bright in the blue sky.

Being on the track with other people is inspiring and amusing. I must have been having a heady morning, feeling pretty good, because when a professional-looking runner came up alongside me, I thought, *Hmm, he's not going that much faster than me.* Only after he sped off into his "real" run did I realize he'd only been warming up.

I'm a move-worms-from-concrete-onto-grass person. A hard rain one night left the track littered and placed me in a moral dilemma: skip the workout, workout and squash the living crap out of them, or workout and save the big ones. Balance in all things, so I chose to use my warm-up laps to clear the bigger ones off. Not sure just how quickly new worms wiggle onto a track, but every time I lapped around, a seeming entirely new cohort had arrived. It was the only time I didn't continue a workout and reverted to saving.

Sometimes, I drive by the track to recall the early sunrises I know I'll enjoy again. Sometimes I just go there in my mind. If something is weighing on me, I think about my workouts, how hard I pushed to complete them, and how much more capable I am than I thought. The track is a grounding point for strength.

Fitness is a lifelong goal. I know the day will come when I'll have to leave the track, the gym, my beloved high-intensity workouts, running, and probably even slow jogs behind. But I want to always be able to bend over, put on some comfy shoes, and go for a walk.

CHAPTER 21

Breaking Barriers

Taking back my health meant breaking barriers that often made me uncomfortable. The more I broke, though, the more I got used to the discomfort. Then I started enjoying the discomfort because I knew it meant something good was happening. And becoming comfortable with discomfort reaches into all parts of life: work, relationships, life's challenges (summoning the courage to contact an internet provider for a service call comes to mind).

PSYCHOLOGICAL BARRIERS

My trainer often says that pushing ourselves is 90 percent *psychological*. If my goal was to run one mile, I started getting tired at three-fourths of a mile. If I was trying to run three miles, I'd get tired at two and a half. In the earlier days, near the end of three or four miles, when I didn't think I could take *one more step*, I'd come to an intersection about to turn red. Rather than running in place while the light changed, I'd have a burst of energy and sprint through. If I was at the end of a five-mile run, feeling like I would fall over if I took one more step, and saw neighbors on their porch, I'd find a burst of energy as I waved while sprinting by them! Knowing there's a reservoir of untapped energy to access is fascinating. Whenever I'm up against something, I know I have more power than I think.

My tactic for fighting the psychological demon? I tell myself to *just hang on*. Whether for one-half loop of a track, one more minute, thirty more steps, *just hang on*. And I always can.

GOING FARTHER

As I got stronger, it was satisfying to go past old turnoff points. Going just a little farther one day, then just a little farther the next. When preparing for my 10-k, pushing my distance to five miles, my route included a park far out of my neighborhood. I felt like I was running to Chicago. Afterward, driving past the park on routine errands and envisioning myself running there felt surreal—and neat.

As I write this, I still can't imagine training for a full (twenty-six-mile) or even half (thirteen) marathon. Who knows what the future might bring? But I know I'll always be able to push myself farther than I could have imagined. And this is true for more than just running.

Fitness is an art and requires finesse. The desire to push myself butts heads with my need to fight excess. My fitness approach has always been steady, safe, sustainable. I temper "going farther" with "just one more"—one more block, lap, set, run up a hill, mile. Today, I did *one more*. Tomorrow, I can do *one more*. Always moving forward but controlling excess.

RUNNING IN THE MORNING

I looked at my trainer like he had green things sticking out of his head when he suggested I try running in the morning before work. The thought of breaking my morning routine seemed unimaginable. But one May morning, I stepped out early into the lovely fresh air, and no surprise, morning workouts are now the most enjoyable part of my day. The early morning almost feels sacred. Like Maria in *The Sound of Music* who, when she wakes up, *wakes up*! I've always sprung out of bed by 5:30, and hours of extra time awaited me. There is nothing, absolutely nothing, more wonderful than opening the door to a soft, fresh, warm morning for an early run. No cars, no fumes, no artificial noise. Just birds singing, bunnies hopping, sun rising. Then home for a shower, healthy breakfast, floating into work and through the day and evening. In winter, when I turn to other workouts and schedules, I have the joy of anticipating the beautiful mornings I know will be there when Earth turns back to the sun.

TRAINING MIDWEEK

My training sessions were always on Saturday mornings. For forty years, I lived in the workweek mindset: work, home, work, home. The thought of a training session during the workweek seemed as foreign as running in the morning. Until I signed up for another series in 2022. With Saturday slots taken, I unhappily chose Wednesdays at 7:30 a.m.

One of the most fun things about life is how it continually surprises. Moving my training sessions to a weekday morning was the best. I enjoy my training sessions whenever they are, but even more so during the week because I have the weekend free, without a to-do list. It's like being a kid again, when you get your homework done on Friday, and the whole weekend is yours. I've occasionally had to select a different morning, but I always knew that the hard work I was putting in during the week would be followed by my *free* weekend. I do solo workouts on weekends in good weather and go to the gym on Sunday mornings in winter. But *it's a choice I'm making*—one of the activities I enjoy and decide to do during my *free* weekend—not a standing "must-do" obligation.

GOING OUT AT NIGHT

It never occurred to me to run at night. Once the sun went down, the door was shut. But that also changed. Running at night is extra special for one reason: stars. Even though I live in a city and know I'm seeing only a fraction of what's up there, seeing any of them in the clear night air is magical. The very best is when I turn certain corners on my route with fewer trees and the sky opens up above me. A $5 headlamp around my neck lights the way just enough for my feet while I look up to marvel at the heavens.

GOING OUT IN WINTER

Going out in cold weather was one of the hardest barriers I had to overcome. Once the temp dropped below forty-five degrees, I was inside. No surprise that now, when it's forty or even thirty-five, I think, *Warm day!* Depending on the surface, I might walk instead of run, but I'm out there. There's something fun about fighting the early winter curfew instead of giving in and feeling like it's time to go to bed at 4 p.m.

Combining winter and nights is especially wonderful because stars are even better in the cold. They seem to glitter more—reflection off the snow? It's always quiet because everyone is snuggled up in their homes. I love solitude—just me and the icy winter stars.

Another nice thing about going out year-round is the feeling of continuity, looking outside my window at snow-covered sidewalks and imagining myself sweating in shorts and a top. Then, six months later, as I head back out to dry concrete streets, remembering how magical they looked covered in soft snow with holiday decoration reflections. As I pass this or that house in summer, I think *Oh, that's the house that puts up the ten-foot candy cane. Oh my god, I wonder what their December electric bill is!*

GOING OUT IN WIND

I love breezes but hate wind—cold or hot. Winter wind is the worst—or used to be. Despite how warmly I'd cover my body, the icy wind attacked my neck (even with my repurposed wide headband to cover it). Then I saw a picture of a skier and discovered the baclava. Two computer clicks and this simple, inexpensive, snuggly piece of polyester transformed my cold-weather life. Neck snug as a bug on even the coldest days. Balaclavas are also great for covering your nose when monster trucks that have somehow escaped emission testing roar past.

Wind in hot weather is also my nemesis but for a different reason: it slows me down! Or so I like to imagine. I feel like I'm running against an eighty-mile-per-hour wind, only to discover it's more like ten (*That can't be right!*). And running with the wind at my back never feels easier. Still can't figure out why *that* is. Reports to my trainer are never complete unless I include the violent winds I persevered through like an Olympic champion.

GOING OUT WHEN I DON'T FEEL LIKE IT

A nice thing about running is that, even if I'm not feeling especially motivated, I can still *do something*. There were times, especially in the early days, when I didn't have the great three- or four-mile run I'd planned. Maybe some crazy pain in my knee or ankle. I'd return home after only running a mile, feeling defeated, but then I would realize, *OMG, I still just ran a mile*! My trainer explained that even professional athletes have off days. But you can always do something. And "somethings" add up.

There were also times when I didn't feel like doing anything because I was distracted. When that happened, I reminded myself that there was not one single more important thing I needed to do than make myself healthier (except watch a new episode of *The Great British Baking Show*).

In 2021, I started keeping a calendar on my kitchen table for jotting down my walks, slow runs, and fast runs: what I did, how far, how long. I love being able to see in one glance what I've done for my body and health in a week or month—even if I didn't always feel like it or wasn't spectacular doing it. And whenever I look at the calendar, I think about what a difference there is between having done even those less-than-perfect things and doing nothing. The thought of what weeks, months, and years of doing nothing would look like was unimaginable.

WORKING THROUGH DISCOMFORT

My trainer says that strengthening a body is about dealing with discomfort. And it's true that the hardest thing for me about training isn't lack of energy or endurance but physical discomfort. This doesn't seem like a profound observation, but it is. Until I became more seasoned, any worry I had about joints or muscles was compounded by my thoughts. *Am I doing more harm than good? Will it always feel this way?* And, the worst, *Am I too old for this?*

Fitness is a complex proposition, a combination of knowing some basic mechanical things (how to stretch, cool down, the right kind of workouts for you) and listening to your body. It was critical to learn the difference between discomfort—the inevitable byproduct of pushing my body toward work-in-progress fitness—and pain—a signal to stop and assess. And how I gauge what I'm feeling versus how someone else would, where I am physically, is subjective. I learned that the clearest marker for distinguishing between discomfort and pain is to determine whether what I'm experiencing is changing the way I'm doing what I'm doing—if it's "changing my form." If I'm running, am I starting to limp? If I'm on a gym machine, am I compensating and not using the machine in the correct way? Having expertise to guide these assessments is the most important benefit of working with a trainer.

My biggest worry was my very non-bionic artificial right

shoulder. Would training further damage it? At the beginning I felt scary sensations, but starting on the elliptical, with those crazy arm handles, allowed me to feel the sensations without fear. My confidence slowly grew to ready me for the weights and strength building to follow. Taking those first steps to strengthen my shoulders allowed me to live an active and relatively worry-free life—something I thought I'd never be able to do again.

My next biggest worry was my ankles. In the early days, they usually always hurt, again making me question if it was "too late" to get healthy. But eventually, my early activities, even if imperfect, started to pay off, and my ankles became stronger. I still would never head out without doing some simple rotations. And sometimes I might feel a twinge here or there as I get going. But whatever's happening works itself out. It makes me feel good to know how much stronger and solid my ankles will be when I'm eighty-five.

In the earlier days, I asked my trainer why my runs felt so good while I was doing them, only to have my knees hurt walking into my house. I was worried that my knees were bad and that it was too late for me to get healthy. But the fix was so simple: I hadn't cooled down, and my hamstrings were tight. That's all it was! This is when I started understanding that most things aren't about bones and joints but the muscles surrounding them.

I came to understand the powerful, positive impact of stretching during cooldowns. My trainer said that most people, even professional runners, warm up but don't like to cool down—the main event is over, and they just want to get on to the next thing. But for me, cooldowns are one of the most enjoyable parts of whatever I've just done. First, it just feels so damn good. Second, I know how much it's helping my muscles. Third, it's so satisfying to stop and take the time—look up at the blue sky, listen to the birds, feel the soft breezes—to contemplate how I'm finally taking care of myself.

Even when doing everything right, my knees still bother me sometimes, and I always dread going along a mile or two just fine and then suddenly feeling tightening and pain, getting sharper. But unless it's so excruciating that I can't go on, unless it makes me want to "change my form," I go on. And somehow, it usually goes away. My continuing work on building strength throughout my hips has significantly reduced knee issues and shows just how connected the parts of our body are.

Side cramps make me feel like I'm going to keel over and die. They're caused by spasms of the diaphragm and seem to pop up out of nowhere. I'm fine one minute, and the next I'm getting stabbed in the side by a knife. To avoid them, my trainer reminded me to breathe normally. This sounded obvious (like when he accurately posited in the early days that my feet were cramping because I was tying my laces too tight—did I think my shoes were going to fall off?). I realized I was producing those gut-wrenching side cramps by breathing unnaturally for two reasons. The first, to try to capture the wonderful, deep, spontaneous breath (the big SB) you get when you run. I'd feel one coming on and breathe harder to try to capture it. But, like the big O, the big SB can't be forced. You have to just keep doing your thing, knowing it's going to come (another ridiculous but must-do bad-pun opportunity) in its own good time. I think the second reason I used to breathe unnaturally was to make myself feel like I was working harder—a clear sign I was ready to increase the intensity of my workouts.

Beyond avoiding side cramps altogether, there *are* strategies to combat them if they do come (ugh!): a good warm-up that includes stretching forward, back, and to the side, to give the diaphragm the same warm-up other muscles get. Some runners put their arms over their head to fight side cramps. I've found, despite everything I just said about breathing naturally, that intentionally breathing in a little more slowly and deeply and holding the breath just a little longer almost always works within half a block or so. I always take time to stretch my torso. I remember the friend I lost to diaphragm cancer when I do.

I have Meige, a dystonia (movement disorder) that causes my facial muscles to move erratically when I talk, eat, or work out.[26] It isn't a common barrier most people confront when learning to work through discomfort. But it's with me all the time—constantly pulling my facial muscles, occasionally making my eyes close until the muscles pull them back open (a challenge for navigating large cracks in the sidewalk). I mention it only because sometimes even I marvel at the focus and determination I seem to have that allows me to put up with it and do it all anyway. I guess the lesson is that there can be many reasons for deciding not to do something, but it only takes one really strong reason to decide to do it.

A NOTE ON ADAMANCY

Taking back my health taught me a profound and valuable lesson: Explore adamancy of any kind and what it might be trying to tell me.

With an 8 a.m. workday start time, I declared to anyone who listened that I just couldn't imagine waiting until 9 a.m. to "start my day." What that reveals about how I thought about my life makes me sad. I jumped into my first full-time job one week after high school and became a work machine. My dad always said that if I worked hard, I'd be rewarded. But that doesn't explain why all I saw for myself in the day was work. Taking back my health returned to me the many hours before heading to an office—and evenings after leaving it. I wish I'd recognized sooner what "waiting to start my day" had subconsciously been trying to tell me.

---

[26] My (low-key) video to educate: https://www.youtube.com/watch?v=52xxLsmSanc

And how often had I adamantly declared to my trainer that "I don't go outside once it gets down to forty," "I don't go outside after it gets dark," "I don't go out if it's windy," or "I'd never schedule a training session in the middle of the week."

As might be expected, overcoming these adamancies improved my health and happiness. Even more than that, I'm now tuned in to adamancy and understand that whenever I sense it, facing and overcoming it will undoubtedly be good for me.

CHAPTER 22

Food Work

I had the motivation and tactics, and I was moving, but there was one other critical element to taking back my health: putting good food in my body. My trainer once said that even though he owned a gym and made his living training people, if someone had to choose between training and eating well to be healthy, he'd tell them to eat well. I've placed this section on food after workouts because, although moving and eating are intertwined, starting to feel the positive effects of moving made changing my food habits easier. I was feeling better and more motivated overall, and knowing I had a certain workout the next day made me think about what I would eat the day before.

In 2019 I explored my relationship to eating. I wanted to take the final step into my "dream" world: living with a sense of control and power and self-esteem and well-being. I wanted to live fully and "perfectly"—being the very best I could be.

When I resumed my training sessions in 2021, even before filling my trainer in on how well I'd fared eating wise during our off months, he said he could tell just by looking at me. But cleaning up my eating was a gradual process.

Even though I'd heard ad nauseam about the importance of eating good food and, through some volunteering, understood its importance for those dealing with depression and bipolar, it took me years to link my food choices with how I felt each day. I now know that when I'd get home from work, feeling worn out, it was in large part because of my food choices, not (necessarily) work.

Feeling great is merely a straightforward mathematical equation: Putting good things in your body equals a better-feeling body. Eat a wide variety of foods that deliver nutrients without excess calories. English nutritionist Amelia Freer made a profound impression on how I think about food, and I still use her food philosophies. I also did some other things.

EAT LESS

I faced an ironic paradox. As the quality and variety of food I ate became more important, I needed to make food *less* important. I always admired people who eat only to subsist. They might even enjoy what they eat, but food isn't the focus of their days. I figured they must be great artists and inventors and people so driven by a passion that food is incidental. In the absence of a driving passion, my challenge was to wrestle with my intrinsic excess tendencies—the primary one being food.

The first thing I focused on to eat less was physical need. A person doesn't need a lot of food to live. We've all experienced getting so caught up in what we're doing that we forget to eat. I spent a couple of days in California eating only strawberries. While staying with a friend in Boston, our dinner was a large bowl of steamed fresh green beans picked from her garden. On days of large work events, I might only have a banana. Eating like this isn't healthy or sustainable, but it demonstrated that I didn't need the amount of food I was taking in. And it made me wonder how my organs could even sustain the huge amounts of food I was shoveling in on a regular basis. Now that I've changed what I eat, I feel fuller sooner—and going over the full line makes me feel uncomfortable and even a little anxious.

The second thing I focused on was emotion. Lots of research has been done on what leads to emotional eating: stress, boredom, compensation. A few years ago, I picked up a medium-sized pizza on a Saturday afternoon. The first couple squares were great. The next were good. The next were all right. But I kept eating even after they stopped tasting like anything. Not sure if I was celebrating something or if there was an emotional issue, but I'd put so much food into my body that I felt sick and even scared. All I could do, literally, was lie on my bed to let whatever was going to happen in my body happen, waiting to recover.

My emotional eating was anchored in happy memories. Those family dinners around the warmly lit table, Mom and Dad and a brother or two, happy conversations, homemade meals. I learned to identify the emotional tug and embrace the memories rather than try to recreate them—knowing they were something to be grateful for and enough on their own. I still have something to eat after work, but it doesn't have to be the full family dinner of my memories or past habits. And although I live with low amounts of stress and boredom, if there is any, I can identify it right away. And then I eat just enough to satisfy and nourish me. And because healthy living doesn't mean perfection, if I do have a tug to eat something, I will in a modest amount.

BECOMING A NATURAL EATER

I also wanted to be a natural eater, letting nature (my body) guide my eating habits. I examined and broke old routines ("if it's noon, I have to stop and eat lunch") and only ate when I was hungry. Because I'm now able to identify emotions that might lead to overeating, I can wait until I feel truly hungry. Feeling genuinely hungry is kind of exciting, kind of primal (knowing, of course, that I'm blessed with having enough to eat). And everything tastes so much better when I'm truly hungry.

Becoming a natural eater also meant figuring out how to

keep from feeling like I was living like a taut rubber band, the tension getting tighter and tighter until one day everything snaps and I'm back to shoveling loads of bad stuff into my mouth. In the past, if a special event was coming up, it was "Quick, go on a diet." I always ended up feeling so deprived that I'd end up eating more and feeling even more lousy than if I hadn't tried to cut back at all. It was almost like self-sabotage, and I never understood it until I recognized it was a real thing: what I call the "deprivation rubber band." Deciding how to avoid it isn't astrophysics; if I eat healthy and naturally most of the time, the tension on the rubber band disappears.

CHANGING MY EATING HABITS

Theories are great but how to actually start changing my habits? Like I do with everything, I made a list of what I was going to eat, do, and not do:

Eat if hungry, stop when full	Oat bran
Protein/fat in the morning	Sorghum
Chicken on weekends	Prunes
Organic foods	Apricots
Sweet potatoes	Ginseng
Less salt/use sea salt	Oils, not pills
Tea, honey, and ginger	800 mgs B6 and B12
Use garlic	Pineapple and kiwi
Omega-3	Carrots
Avocado/walnuts	Unbleached products
Apple	No canned food
Brown rice	No processed food
Blueberries	Vitamins/fish oil
No butter	Raisins for sweet
Broccoli	Less bread

Homemade soup	Less dessert
Whole oats	Less salad bar
Water purifier	Small, healthier choices
Chew slowly	Weights, once a week
Sesame seeds/oil	Steel oats with blueberries
Apple cider vinegar	Less junk food and snacks
Dark grapes	No more subs

It was a good list—although still not quite there: no dessert instead of "less" dessert; no junk food instead of "less" junk food. But it was a clear and cohesive way, a point of departure, to seriously think about my health and the relatively painless daily activities I could improve.

Some truths:

- You can eat an unbelievably large amount of good food.
- To eat well, you have to have good food around.
- There are lots of easy and satisfying substitutes for bad food.
- When you've eaten good food for a while, bad food tastes really bad. The next time you drive past a fast-food place, notice the grease in the air.
- If you eat good food most of the time, you can have anything *once in a while*.
- Taking time to prepare good food is one of the most satisfying parts of the day.

HELLO FOOD PREPPING

The first thing I did was overhaul my pantry, a drudge task that was unexpectedly enjoyable. I put on music, settled in for the duration, and looked at the contents of anything in my freezer, refrigerator, shelves, and spice cabinet. If it was bad for me, it left the building. After the scour, I had about a third of what I'd started with, but I felt exhilarated.

I had only healthy food around, but there wasn't much variety, so I hit my healthy cookbooks. I also invested in quality freezer containers. Making vegetable lasagna while listening to the radio is a relaxing and satisfying way to spend a Sunday afternoon. I can enjoy a good Sunday evening dinner, some leftovers, and individually freeze future dinners. A simple thing like buying those frozen tins radically changed my meal habits.

I also got in the habit of prepping for the week. I'd seen articles about how serious athletes prepare a week's meals in advance. This sounded like another drudge task but became another of my favorite parts of the weekend—often done while my lasagna or some other dish bakes. I boil a dozen eggs, cut carrots into strips, and reduce a head of cauliflower into bite-size pieces. Everything is placed in containers, and for work lunches, I take a few of each to accompany a peanut butter sandwich made with my homemade bread, piece of fruit, yogurt, a handful of walnuts, and half a cup of low-fat cottage cheese. I pretty much eat the same thing every day and never get tired of it because it tastes so good. When I start to get hungry around 11:30 (because I rise and eat breakfast early), nothing tastes better than that sandwich, veggies, and tahini.[27]

SO LONG, CHEESE AND CANDY

I never gave things up for Lent, but in 2019 I decided to forgo cheese and candy. One of my first "fifteen-minute" (forty-day) goals.

Lots of people say they "enjoy cheese"—the graceful cheese connoisseurs, going to the public market and chatting with cheese vendors, trying samples, exploring exotic varieties, trying

---

[27] Instead of slathering my veggies in ranch dressing like I used to, I make a batch of tahini dip that I heard a chef call her go-to: equal parts apple cider vinegar, tahini, extra virgin olive oil, and liquid aminos. The chef used soy sauce, but liquid aminos has less sodium. Also good for salad dressing and brushing on salmon.

it in recipes, cutting off a bite-sized piece here and there. I'm not one of those people. My name is Kathy, and I am a cheese addict. I can finish off a large block of cheddar in two or three days. Cheese calls out to me from the refrigerator: "*Kathy*, I'm right over *here*. Stop whatever you're doing *immediately* and come have another *piece* of me." I also came to suspect that cheese was making me congested, although I'd been too lazy to confirm that in a systematic, scientific way. I also knew that cheese, like a filet o' fish, might as well get glued directly onto my thighs.

I also gave up candy. Like cheese, once I start eating candy, I can't stop. One Hershey's Kiss leads to a mountain of them. One snack size Snickers leads to ten.

When Lent ended, I'd seen how easy giving them both up had been and didn't go back. But again, to make my choices sustainable over the long-term and avoid the deprivation rubber band, I compromised and began buying a hard piece of Parmesan to shred. Too much work for snacking, but there if needed.

There's no great substitute for candy (although Turkish apricots are pretty damn good). I made it a little over a year before I was tempted by a mini Hershey bar, and I was shocked by how disappointingly fake and chemically it tasted. The relapse was temporary because I'd learned what sugar was doing to my body. I only relent annually at Halloween, and it's like being a kid again, "waiting" for the treat. Reese's—of course. But the day after, when the ghouls and goblins have transformed back into children, any leftovers leave the house.

It's still not always easy, and sometimes when shopping, I gaze down the endless row of *cheese*. But seeing so much of it in one place seems to make it less special and easier to pass up.

SO LONG, PASTA

One of my favorite things will always be egg noodles slathered in butter and salt. This was a daily after-school snack for a friend and me at her house. It is beyond embarrassing to admit that I once asked her mom, "What kind of noodles do you buy?" in hopes of prompting an offer (sigh). I can only pray I've gotten brighter.

My love affair with pasta began when I was seven or eight. A friend had a stove in her basement, and we boiled water to make elbow macaroni. We felt like the French Chef. Sixty years later, I can still taste that macaroni: watery and bland. And wonderful.

Fast-forward fifty years, and I was boiling one hell of a lot of pasta. Sometimes with just butter and salt, sometimes "made healthy" by adding tomatoes, tomato sauce (full of sugar), and basil—and butter and salt. *Lots* of butter and salt. I ate three times what a single portion would be. When I began eating healthier, I started using kosher salt and olive oil instead of butter. A little better health-wise and still tastes pretty good.

I gave up pasta soon after the Lent cheese/candy experiment. After changing some other simple food habits, I'd noticed how bloated it made me feel. Like the cheese and candy, I was surprised at how easy it was to give up.

The only pasta I still use (and only occasionally) is for lasagna: Gardein meatless crumbles, spinach, carrots, zucchini, spices, Parmesan, tomato sauce. Super good and still reasonably healthy. Like the cheese and candy, I'd figured out a way to still have pasta once in a while and avoid the deprivation rubber band.

SO LONG, BUTTER

I slathered butter on more than pasta. And no surprise that I mean *tablespoons* of butter. I buried baked potatoes in it and then, to get healthier, buried sweet potatoes in it. Olive oil can be used instead of butter on a surprising number of things. I was too cheap to buy Lidia's fancy oil but wanted to go one step up from store-brand and found California Olive Ranch Extra Virgin Olive Oil Global Blend. Great on vegetables, especially with a sprinkling of kosher salt. Now I only eat two tablespoons of butter on my weekly just-out-of-the-oven homemade bread. Butter was so much easier to leave behind than I would have thought. That said, if I'm going to eat "butter," I eat real butter.

HELLO, PROTEIN

I spent thirty years protein starved. I worked second shift in the eighties and early nineties, and for many of those years, my "dinner" was at 3 p.m. and consisted of two slices of canned Dole pineapple rings and a piece of toasted bread topped with two slices of American cheese and onions. I thought this was a pretty healthy meal (fruit, wheat bread, cheese, and onion), but I was really eating sugar syrup, preserved carbohydrates, and fake cheese. I guess the onions were okay. And all of it metabolized within a couple of hours, leaving me empty midshift and heading downstairs to the vending machine for some kind of terrible, fake fast-food to heat up that only poured more empty calories into my body. I didn't know a thing about protein and how critical it is to health—one of the most important benefits being to leave me feeling full and satisfied.

Any amount of protein I did eat was reduced even more when I stopped eating red meat in the early 2000s. It's the usual story. Driving on the freeway, I looked over at a truck packed with cows peering out of the slats. It still bothers me to think about how scary it must be for chickens and turkeys when they're being processed, but it's got to be especially scary for large animals. Vegetarian combinations of legumes and beans to create a full protein never caught on with me because, as delicious as the meals were, I never finished them, and they don't store well.

But I needed more protein. I'd never spent a lot of money on meat (the image of Mary Tyler Moore grimacing as she plops the meat into her grocery cart stuck), and even buying chicken or turkey seemed like an extravagance.

I started with fish. I worked with a woman who was repelled by fish, describing them as cold-blooded creatures with scales that swim around in God-knows-what kind of water. I can see it. But I'd also had enough good meals with fish and dove in (a pretty good pun, I think).

HELLO, SHRIMP

At the holidays, my mom would splurge on a large bowl of fresh shrimp to enjoy as we gathered around the table. And I'd had my share of good breaded shrimp over the years. But it had fallen out of my awareness until my sister offered me a frozen bag of it—which sat in my freezer because I had no idea what to do with it. Then I saw a *Lidia's Kitchen* episode that featured an easy recipe for shrimp and zucchini. After seeing how good and easy it was, I used it often. But cleaning and preparing the shrimp was tedious, and I was too cheap to buy it fresh.

HELLO, SALMON

Growing up, I'd only had the salmon canned in oil that you had to pull the bones out of (yuck). But it was a "delicacy" for us, and I liked it. As an adult, I wandered in the Salmon Desert for forty years until the late 2000s, when a dining companion ordered it. The thought of ordering something like that when there were so many "better" things on the menu seemed odd. But curiosity won out, and I ordered it too. It was a fancy restaurant, the salmon was fantastic, and I saw the light.

My favorite salmon meal was at a now-closed local place: perfectly seasoned and cooked, just a hint of sear, alongside garlic mashed potatoes (life *is* short). The thought of preparing it myself was still daunting, though, so I started buying it frozen. I had it once or twice a month for about a year until I noticed that the pieces seemed to be getting smaller, making me recognize it for what it was: a boxed, mass-marketed, kind-of-but-not-really-healthy product, and I finally made the change to fresh. The slightly higher price for the real thing seemed worth leaving the preservatives and other synthetic additives behind. Every couple of months, I buy four filets at a time that I freeze individually.

I began making my own salmon in the oven—baking the crap out of it until it looked like a piece of shoe leather to make sure it was cooked. Then, on a cooking show, I saw how easy it is to prepare in a pan (slowly) and never looked back. This isn't a cookbook, but one of my favorite things to do is marinate the filet in a mixture of molasses, ketchup, mustard, kosher salt, a tiny touch of apple cider vinegar, and a dash of pepper. Save a tablespoon for brushing over the top when it's almost done. *Yum.*

GOODBYE, BREAD. HELLO, BREAD.

Salmon is even better when it's topped with homemade seasoned breadcrumbs. One of the smartest things I ever did was learn to make my own bread. My dad learned when he retired. His first loaf was such a misshapen mass of hard tack that he painted it with shellac, my mom tied a red ribbon around it, and it became a beloved piece of family lore—serving as our front door stop. But boy did he learn—French, rye, white—fluffy and light as a feather. I can still taste the soft warm slices of his bread slathered in butter.

For thirty years, I'd thought about making my own bread, but it always seemed too hard or too complicated, and I couldn't imagine having the patience to do something in steps: doing one thing, waiting, doing something else, waiting. But I finally got tired of paying for and throwing away unused store-bought bread filled with unnatural ingredients. So I found a recipe for simple white bread and, like Sir Edmund Hilary, courageously began climbing the bread-baking mountain.

In the beginning, I tenaciously (and nervously) clung to the recipe and had some definite hits and misses. Now, of course, I can make it in my sleep. Not sure my humble loaves are bakery quality, but every week, I have a delicious work lunch with my homemade creation that doesn't contain chemicals and costs practically nothing. Oh, and the personal satisfaction.

The real treat is waiting fifteen minutes for it to cool, cutting off both ends, and dipping them in oil olive and herbs or treating myself to those two tablespoons of butter. Another super treat? Even though I halve the recipe, I still usually can't finish an entire loaf before it passes its prime. So, every Sunday, I cut the leftover pieces into small croutons, cover them in olive oil and herbs, and bake for ten minutes. Voilà, a great crunchy snack for late afternoon cravings. The teeny, tiniest crumbs are added to a container, put in the freezer, and sprinkled on top of my salmon with a touch of olive oil. Delicious. I can have my bread and eat it too.

HELLO, ORANGES

Eating an orange is like eating a piece of the sun. At buffets, I always headed for the vegetables. Most fruit tasted sour to me, and cantaloupe tasted like mold (still does). My mom mentioned once how much she liked fruit, and her casual comment stayed with me. When I seriously started changing what I ate, discovering fruit was like discovering a new frontier of deliciousness: bananas (just ripe), apples (McIntosh), sweet pineapple, and wonderful deep purple grapes that look like fingers and taste like candy.

But I'd still never dared to try oranges again—too many memories of pale, sour orbs full of seeds—until Christmas 2019, when my brother offhandedly commented that oranges (his favorite food) didn't seem to be as good that year. I'll never understand how the mind works, but four months later, his comment made me try one, and I was hooked. I don't know if oranges are grown differently these days, if they're genetically modified, or if my mom just bought lousy ones, but today's oranges aren't the ones she used to get. For the past couple of years, I've eaten at least one a day, sometimes two, occasionally three. I eat so many of them, sometimes my fingers hurt from peeling them. During the recent supply chain issue, I almost felt panicky when they were low at the store, and I'd buy two bags just to make sure I had some. It's like I can't get the pieces in my mouth fast enough—juicy, sweet, heaven dripping down my chin. Oranges: nature's Snickers.

HELLO, AVOCADOS

I'd marry an avocado if I could. Not sure what we were talking about, but in the mid-2000s, my hair stylist mentioned how much she liked them. I didn't give them another thought until, fifteen years later, at a work potluck, someone made an avocado, tomato, onion, and cilantro dip topped with kosher salt. It was all I ate at that potluck, and by 2020, I replaced my morning store-bought bread and butter with half an avocado, a pinch of kosher salt, and protein-packed hemp hearts. Avocados are much easier to use than I'd thought. I buy a few green ones, leave one on the counter, and put the others in the fridge. In a day, the one on the counter is perfect. I cut it in two lengthwise, rotate, wrap the half with the pit in foil, and put it back in the fridge. You can spoon out perfect chunks. The next day, when I take out the second half, I put one more on the counter. Perfectly ripe avocados every day. I can feel my doctor jumping for joy as my good HDL rises.

HELLO, YOGURT

Yogurt was another of those "exotic" things I'd never thought of eating. A Greek high school friend ate "real" yogurt. I tried hers once, hated it, and didn't think about it again. In the mid-1990s, I noticed a container sitting on someone's desk in the sun (*bleech*) and recoiled anew. But sometime in the late 2000s, I discovered Yoplait (cherry flavor). I must have internalized the Jamie Lee Curtis commercials (score one for marketing), and I ate that kind for many years.

As I began refining what I put in my body, the amount of sugar in Yoplait started to bother me, and I turned to Dannon Light and Fit—eighty calories, nine grams of sugar. My favorites: cherry, blueberry, strawberry/banana. I didn't fool myself into believing it met authentic Greek yogurt standards, but it's what I was willing to settle on—knowing it was relatively healthy and liking it enough to make it a routine part of my eating.

Eventually, I came to settle on Oikos Pro—twenty grams of protein, no added sugar. I usually also have yogurt with my homemade croutons.

HELLO, OATMEAL

I ate bad breakfasts for years. That piece of store-bought refined "wheat" bread (wheat means healthy, right?) topped with butter and a packet of Quaker Oats instant oatmeal. It was easy, tasted good, and, after all, it was "oatmeal." My trainer's *good food* list included homemade rolled oats. I couldn't imagine taking the time each morning to make real oatmeal, especially during the five years I had the 8 a.m. start time with the fifty-minute one-way drive.

I finally took the leap and, of course, couldn't believe how fast and easy making real oatmeal is. I make double and put leftovers in the refrigerator—just as good heated up the next day. Add frozen blueberries after thirty seconds in the microwave, cinnamon, a few chopped walnuts, and you're in blueberry pancake heaven. Instead of empty calories and artificial ingredients, I now have a deliciously satisfying breakfast that's making me healthy. And a box of eight Quaker Oats packets that lasts eight days is $3.39, while a bag of sixteen-ounce rolled oats that lasts two months is $8. Oatmeal—it's what's for breakfast.

HELLO, SPICES

I didn't have much exposure to spices growing up. My dad had ulcers, and in the days before we knew they're caused by bacteria, my mom kept food simple. Spaghetti with ground beef and tomato sauce. The only thing spices meant to me was wasted money. If I had to get one or two for a recipe, the rest expired until I needed them again and had to buy more.

My pantry sweep had included spices, and I started using small bulk amounts from Outpost Natural Foods. It felt good to know that my spice cabinet, which gradually increased as I continued trying new recipes, was refilled with fresh samples that smelled wonderful, tasted great, and were good for me.

I wish I had more success growing and drying herbs, but it hasn't happened (yet). I do my pre-flowering harvest, tie and hang the clump of beautiful fragrant basil—only to crush and have it taste like cardboard. Buying my herbs in bulk is cost effective, easy, and satisfying.

SAVORY CRAVINGS: WALNUTS

Walnuts are my snack of choice. They were always part of our family Christmas—sitting around a big wooden bowl brimming with them and almonds, pecans, and hazelnuts—each of us armed with our own old-fashioned iron nutcracker that never quite worked. Now I have Christmas year-round by buying big bags from the baking section. They're loaded with fat, the good kind, and I have a handful every day. A satisfying and healthy savory snack.

SWEET CRAVINGS: DRIED APRICOTS AND PICKLES

When I crave something sweet, one dried apricot does the trick. Satisfying to chew and full of fiber. They're also good chopped up into chicken salad (with walnuts—of course). I can't recall how I discovered small sweet gherkin pickles, but just one also satisfies sweet cravings immediately. Probably not as healthy as a dried apricot but still better than the hundreds of other things I could grab. I couldn't even guess how many extra calories these two simple things have saved my body from.

SWEET CRAVINGS: PROTEIN SHAKES

There are 500,000 recipes for smoothies. I use one: almond milk, protein powder, a tablespoon of peanut butter, and a banana (or strawberries). This simple formula gives me more of the crucial protein I need, takes less than two minutes to make, and tastes *great*. If I'm tempted to head to Leon's for two scoops of butter pecan ice cream (one of the best things about Milwaukee), I instead whip up one of these shakes and feel completely satisfied.

HELLO, VITAMINS AND MINERALS

Vitamins and minerals . . . nap time. But they're actually fascinating. My eighth-grade Home Economics (now called Family and Consumer Sciences) teacher could have made learning about them a hell of a lot more interesting. The boring, rote explanations and memorization of random letters, some with weird, pesky numbers, didn't begin to capture how interesting they are. I'm not sure how I would have presented them, but it'd be something like this: Vitamins and minerals are fascinating biological substances that make our miraculous bodies work better. But I don't kid myself. What teenager cares about that?

Thinking about whether I was getting the right kind and number of vitamins and minerals was an important goal. But figuring it out also became a game. It was fun to see "how I stacked up" in a given day, like reaching levels in a video game.

I'd gotten interested enough to try to create some handmade tools. I printed stuff from the web, cutting and taping it into a more usable version for myself, trying to find the right levels for each. It got so complicated that I never finished the project.

Then I discovered Cronometer, the free online food tracker. I entered what I ate, and the breakdowns appeared magically before me—levels of every element, which foods contributed to each, the percentages, and alerts for high levels. It's easy to use because their library is vast, down to particular brands and types, and there are multiple choices for amounts (e.g., I can change one tablespoon to three). Once I got on the solid road to healthy eating and knew what I was consuming, I didn't need to keep using it. I revisit it here and there—like when I began a high protein diet and wanted to see how things were adding up. It's a fascinating tool and one I never could have recreated even with my trusty paper and ruler.

No synthetic vitamins or minerals beat real nutritious food, but I do take some supplements. It pains me to think about how (like "joggers") I got sucked into the mean comments floating around in the late seventies: "He's a pill popper." Why the ridicule? What in the world could have been wrong with taking vitamins? Just because it was new or different? I try to be easy on myself, understanding that we react according to who we are at any given time. But it saddens me to think I was so easily caught up in the social snideness around me. Over the years, I've thought about the jogger and pill popper phenomena—determined never to let myself be swayed by popular opinion about anything again.

For supplements, I went back and forth for years between

what was the latest thing and what was on sale, finally settling on a quality women's multivitamin and fish oil (and a niacinamide capsule to ward off damage from teenage years spent frying in the sun slathered in baby oil). Every morning, as I fill my glass half full of water (always half *full*), it feels good to take them, knowing they're serving me as they should: as supplements to my healthy eating.

I might not have implemented everything on my brainstorming list (I still have no idea what sorghum is, and have you seen the cost of pine nuts?), but making fundamental changes to what I put in my body was easy, and it changed how my body felt and how I felt about my body.

PART V

NEVER GOING BACK

CHAPTER 23

The Tipping Point

It took ten years, but by 2023, my war with excess to take back my health finally brought me to the *tipping point*—the place where I'd never go back to feeling bad. At the tipping point, everything has come together: the enlightened mind, structured physical fitness, the best nutrition, feeling strong, and coming to enjoy all of it. And, above all, realizing that none of it had been all that hard.

The tipping point is a popular catchphrase these days, but I learned about it forty-five years ago, again from Nan Gilbert's *The Unchosen*.[28] Ellen had starved herself to prepare to meet her pen-pal boyfriend. Getting back on track, she embarked on a steady and controlled self-improvement plan (healthy eating, exercise, grooming, tending to her wardrobe, other daily tasks). After another pen-pal disappointment, she vowed not to waste any more time on her new routine. What had it all been for anyway? She decided she would go back to her old life. Then she sat up in bed with a new thought: *What if the old life doesn't fit anymore?* Ellen had reached her tipping point.

Five stages of change brought me to mine:

---

[28] Nan Gilbert, *The Unchosen* (Ishi 2015).

Stage 1 Unaware	Stage 2, 2012 Becoming Aware	Stage 3, 2013-16 Unstructured Work
• not thinking about health	• noticing how lousy I felt • taking no action • things I'd noticed start bubbling up	• starting to feel a little better • fragmented attempts (moving but eating bad food) • limited knowledge • fragmented momentum (starting and stopping) • wondering if people are noticing

Stage 4, 2017-22 Precarious Structured Work	Stage 5, 2023 Tipping Point
• starting to feel good • less fragmentation (moving more and eating better) • learning more • increasing momentum (more consistency) • seeking outside validation	• feeling great • no fragmentation (putting it all together) • knowing what to do • constant momentum (solid routine) • outside validation not needed

As solid as the tipping point is, it's still not a guarantee. It will always be too easy to revert to a bad decision from time to time. But it's the "time to time" that's the difference. The tipping point isn't about perfection. It's about never going back.

Undergirding the tipping point is creating a healthful food practice that can be sustained and avoids the deprivation rubber band. Every February, will I buy a three-pack of strawberry cream puffs from the Wisconsin State Fair Valentine's Day drive-through? Count on it.

Every March, will I slide a sleeve of Thin Mint Girl Scout cookies into my mouth—probably all at once? Absolutely.

And come to my house on Halloween for Reese's.

As Amelia Freer says, I don't need to be perfect. I just need to be good most of the time. Making daily, small, good decisions was much easier once I reached the tipping point. I've moved beyond the day-to-day battles with willpower. I know I'm going to have Thin Mints in March and Reese's at Halloween. But I also know with dead certainty that I'm not going to eat all the other junk that comes flying at me every day. The dead certainty makes temptation irrelevant.

I knew I'd reached the tipping point during a vacation, standing in front of a hotel breakfast buffet. I'd always used being on vacation as an excuse to load up my plate with the calorie-ridden blueberry breads, muffins, and scones. Only after I returned home did I realize I hadn't even considered choosing those things. No more fighting with myself over what I'm going to put in my body, no more temptation. The Promised Land.

The tipping point doesn't guarantee I won't continue to be battered with worldly circumstances. But it does guarantee I won't be flung around this way and that in the health storm of life. The tipping point is my rudder, and I always know which way I'm going: ahead.

CHAPTER 24

A Note on Choices

The best choice I made for my health was to work with a professional trainer. The second best was changing my professional work.

I left a grant manager position at a large federal health center in southeast Wisconsin for an executive assistant position at a small nonprofit in Milwaukee with a significantly lower salary. The justification for accepting the lower salary was shifting from a fifty-minute commute (each way) and 8 a.m. start time to an eleven-minute commute with a 9 a.m. start time. But the move became much more. Being in an organization I'm proud of, working with dedicated people, is definitely special. But the shorter commute and 9 a.m. start time opened up a world of fitness options that helped me take back my joy. The money I gave up was nothing compared to the other riches I found.

CHAPTER 25

A Note on Reverence

Taking back my health would require the one extra thing I'd struggled with my whole life: learning to treat my body with love and care instead of defaulting to excess and using it as a workhorse.

I'd heard the *body is a temple* analogy countless times, but physical self-reverence doesn't have to be that grand. My body is simply an amazingly strong yet fragile tool to carry me through my time in this world. My health work helped me learn to care for it as one would a child. To marvel at it. To embrace it. To respect it. To listen to it. To rest and rejuvenate it. To be kind to it. To love it. *To ask for help*.

This is the part of the book where I share my *stunning after photo:*

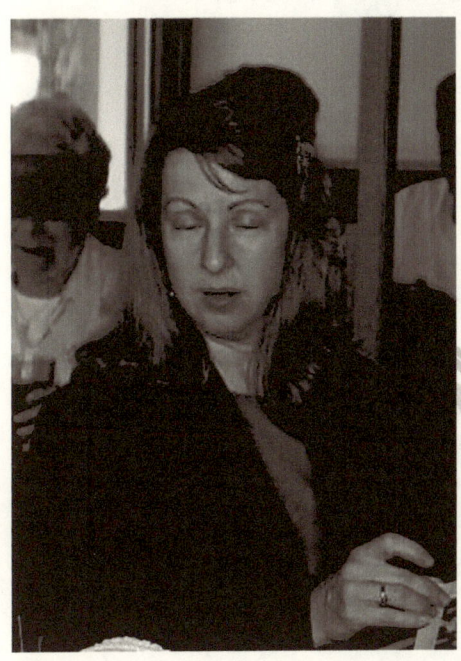 

Sixty-six years old and five shoulder surgeries later.
Liking how I look but loving how I feel.

Photo credit (right): Maureen M Kane of MMK Design, LLC

CHAPTER 26

Patient, Slow, Steady: Forever

Fighting excess to take back my health taught me to be patient, slow, and steady, freeing myself from the cravings and abuse that dominated so much of my early life, feeling my esteem rise as I slogged to the gym in the dead of winter, seeing how my efforts were always moving forward until finally, finally, finally, seeing how my body was meant to look.

Patient, slow, steady led to sustainable.

Patient, slow, steady changed every area of my life.

Patient, slow, steady brought me the best kind of peace there is—the kind I made for myself.

APPENDIX A

Shoulder Surgery Survival Tips for the Single Person

PAPERWORK

- Confirm coverage and status of deductibles with your insurance.
- Obtain and prepare required paperwork ahead of time.
- Try to have one-on-one contact with your doctor's office staff when processing paperwork.
- Make a copy of all paperwork for your files.
- Make follow-up calls to ensure that all parties have processed and/or received required paperwork.

THE KITCHEN

- Put heavy items on the counter before the surgery.
- Pre-open jars and packaged food.
- Make a shopping list and stock up.
- Grocery delivery services are a good way to obtain fresh foods (fruits and vegetables).
- If you do not have someone cooking for you, prepare meals in advance and freeze in small quantities.

YOUR HOME

- TV trays work well for holding needed items.
- A collection of different-sized pillows will be useful.

STAYING BUSY

- Have light books and materials on hand.
- Develop a varied routine to fight boredom.
- Let yourself relax and heal. Your work will be there!

GENERAL

- Make a list of questions in preparation for doctor visits.
- Stock up on pet food and litter.
- Pain medications can affect the elimination system. Eat fruit and stay hydrated.
- If you don't use transportation, research bus schedules.

GROOMING/DRESSING

- Use button-up clothing.
- Have a supply of large bandages and hydrocortisone.
- Use medium-sized towels.
- Taping a razor onto a long-handled object will make grooming easier.
- Set your toothbrush in a cup for easy toothpaste application.

PHYSICAL THERAPY

- Large frozen bags of corn or stir fry conform around your shoulder nicely.
- Give yourself time to heal. Just because you can do something doesn't mean you should do it.
- It's when you begin to feel "good" that you need to be most careful to not overdo it!

www.ingramcontent.com/pod-product-compliance
Lightning Source LLC
LaVergne TN
LVHW042248070526
838201LV00089B/75